The journey you are about to embark upon will transform your mind & body.

All of us struggle to some degree with health, fitness, and wellness during our lives. Move Forward encourages you to fall in love with the power and magic of movement.

Throughout my career, as a movement expert, I have witnessed the power and magic of movement. Everything from back pain to immediate pain relief, walking with a cane to walking independently, unable to get off the ground to able to get off the ground, poor posture to neutral spine, no confidence to radiating confidence, lacking the strength to stronger all around, poor core stability to tremendous core stability, impaired muscle activation to reflexive activation, fragile to injury resilient, medicated to non-medicated, poor metabolic health to metabolically healthy, unmotivated to motivated, high body mass index to normal body mass index, poor bone mineral density to normal bone mineral density, high blood pressure to normal blood pressure, mindlessness to mindfulness, hopeless to hopeful, shameful to proud, near-death to living purposefully, and finally self-centered to impacting others.

When you follow science-based systems, you get predictable results. When you apply the brilliance of consistency, you experience progress and ultimately, the magic of movement.

Move Forward represents the most compelling fitness system ever created. In the worst-case scenario, Move Forward may provide a starting point or Gold standard for the unregulated fitness industry. I can say that with confidence because none of the components are mine. The components are a collection of some of the most influential and respected minds and systems within the fitness industry. You'll soon learn more about those pioneers, their specialties, and most importantly how to integrate their recommendations into your life.

Embrace strategic movement and remain open-minded to what may be better than what you are currently doing.

Stay strong and trust the process,

Korey McCoy

Korey McCoy, M.S.

MOVE FORWARD

21BOOM

Korey McCoy, M.S.

TM and Copyright © 2022 Korey McCoy, M.S.
21BOOM, Plan 4 Fitness, LLC.
For permissions contact: Admin@21-Boom.com
Visual Concept and Graphic Design by Jesus A. Rodriguez C.
All rights reserved.

No part of this book may be reproduced in any manner whatsoever without the prior written permission of the publisher, except in the case of brief quotations embodied in reviews.

The views and opinions expressed in this book are those of the author and do not necessarily reflect the official policy or position of Halo Publishing International. Any content provided by our authors are of their opinion and are not intended to malign any religion, ethnic group, club, organization, company, individual or anyone or anything.

ISBN: 978-1-63765-219-0
LCCN: 2022905901

Halo Publishing International, LLC
www.halopublishing.com

Printed and bound in the United States of America

Contents

FOREWORD	7
PREFACE	9
WHAT IS MOVE FORWARD?	10
WHO ARE YOU?	12
MOVE FORWARD: A MINDSET	14
HEALTH & MOVEMENT FIRST	17
IS THIS YOUR CALL TO ACTION?	21
A MECHANISM FOR EXTRAORDINARY LIVING	22
COLLEEN LEONARD CASE STUDY	62
FIVE LIFESTYLE BEHAVIORS TO OPTIMIZE	65
ASCEND MILESTONES	87
COLLABORATION AND ACCOUNTABILITY THROUGH CONNECT SESSIONS	120
THE MOVE FORWARD INFOGRAPHIC	122
START AND FINISH STRONG	123
THE 7-DAY BEHAVIORAL BLUEPRINT	126
DISCLAIMER AND MEDICAL ADVICE	131
EXERCISE GALLERY	134
MILESTONE INFOGRAPHIC	220

21 BOOM

MOVE FORWARD

Korey McCoy, M.S.

FOREWORD

In my first book, *Your Performance Journey*, professional coaches are the intended audience. *Your Performance Journey* identifies the systems we use, compares the pros and cons of different exercise types, and introduces the navigation system and milestones necessary for a body transformation. Although the information, specifically the milestones, are similar, *Move Forward* has been written to help anyone experience progress, reach their potential, and live an extraordinary life. *Move Forward* is a valuable resource for those not exercising, those sporadically exercising, or those looking for a path to their potential.

As you read this book, you'll notice the term *21BOOM*. *21* stands for the *21* Milestones that personalize the movement experience, and BOOM is an acronym for Behavioral Optimization Online Motivator. 21BOOM is a scalable, online, and interactive wellness platform for clients, coaches, and organizations interested in optimal health, graceful aging, and extraordinary living.

I believe you have three universal health, fitness, and wellness rights, regardless of age, fitness level, experience, or income level.

You have the RIGHT to:

#1: A Personalized, Body-Friendly, and Science-Based Wellness Approach

#2: Guidance and Support on Your Journey

#3: An Online Platform to Educate and Track Your Progress

You can review more at

https://www.21-boom.com.

PREFACE

Most of us are in constant pursuit of personal and professional growth. With all the experts, knowledge, and information at our fingertips, why are so many of us struggling? Why is the health data pointing to more significant problems with stress, depression, and obesity? I don't pretend to have all the answers to these questions. However, I do offer a straightforward mechanism for personal growth and life balance. This mechanism creates a somatic transformation when practiced.

Somatic transformation is a body-centered, relational methodology based on interpersonal neural psychology and ancient wisdom. This program is a roadmap to activate a reflexive mind-body connection. It is incredibly exciting to be able to present this framework, which incorporates a wide range of systems to work in harmony for optimal results.

In essence, I have been a wellness and movement expert for thirty years, and our team has changed the lives of thousands. Today, it is your turn to begin your journey to extraordinary living!

Are you the absolute best version of yourself? Are you taking the small steps necessary to lead an extraordinary life? There are many paths to your potential. Most of us never choose a path; we float down the river of life, ending at an ocean of pain, discomfort, and health-related issues. *Move Forward* represents a path well taken. You'll experience physical and emotional growth as you execute the specific actions within *Move Forward*.

WHAT IS MOVE FORWARD?

I remember the exact day, minute, and moment I reached rock bottom. At that moment, I experienced hopelessness. Hopelessness was a feeling that was so empty, so void of purpose, it left me questioning life itself. Hopelessness sits on the extreme end of the happiness continuum, and at that moment, I only had three options: to end my life, to remain paralyzed and powerless, or to Move Forward!

I'll get into how I arrived at hopelessness a bit later. More importantly, how did I overcome hopelessness to thrive? I chose to Move Forward! The choice to Move Forward is primarily a mindset. In fact, the greatest gift is a mindset shift.

Move Forward means progress.

Move Forward creates clarity.

Move Forward is a navigation mechanism to extraordinary living.

Move Forward at the root begins with physiology and human movement.

> "Even more fundamental to our performance than thinking or feeling is our raw emotion. You have to change the emotion, to change the feeling, to change the thinking to ultimately change how you behave. Finally, beyond emotion, we get to the very heart of the matter (if you'll excuse the pun). We get to our physiology. If you want to be brilliant every day and achieve higher levels of performance, it is essential to go much deeper than behavior and get right down to our physiology." —Excerpt from Coherence: The Secret Science of Brilliant Leadership by Dr. Alan Watkins

HERE'S A POWERFUL GRAPHIC FROM THAT EXPERT:

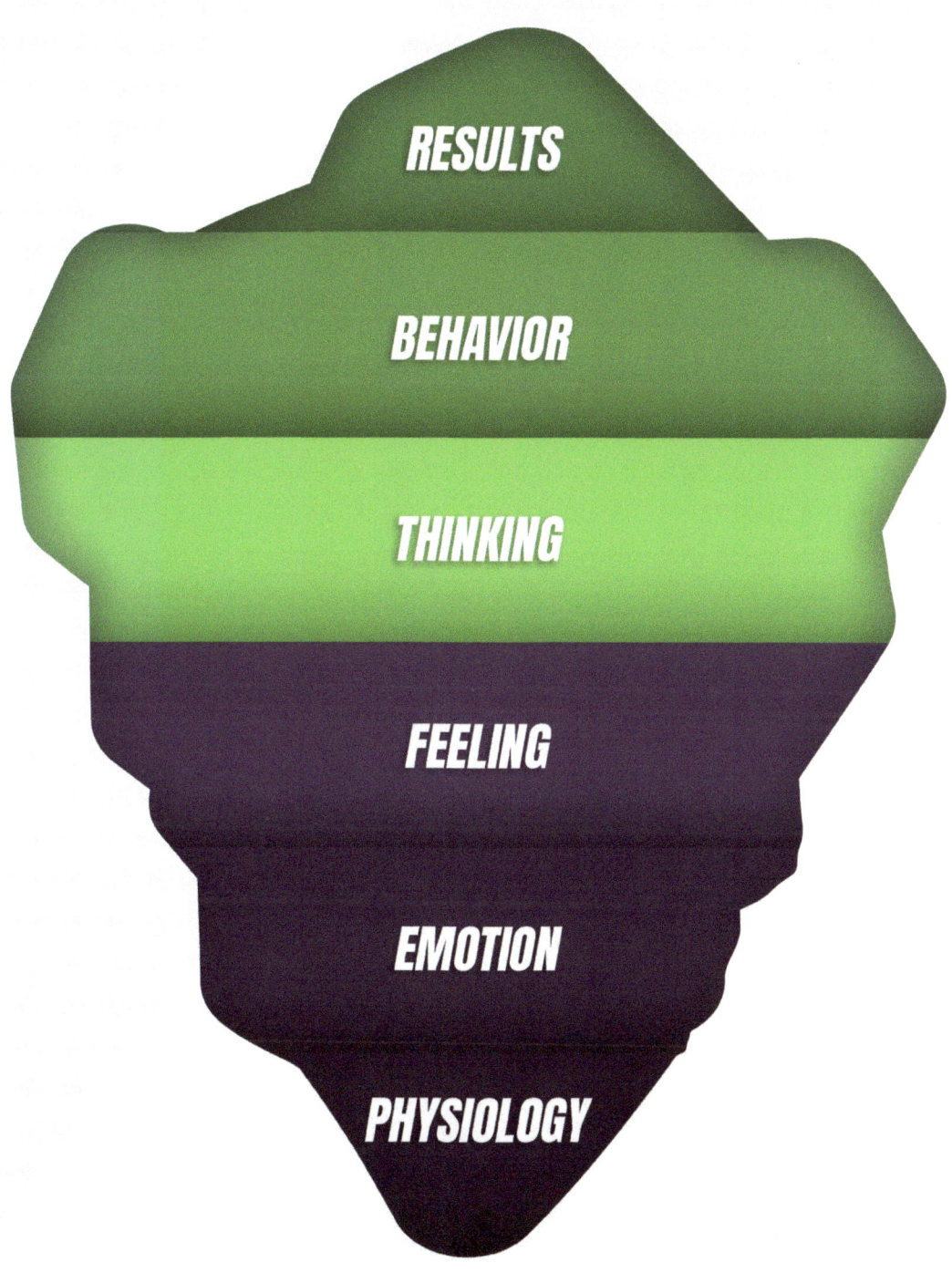

WHO ARE YOU?

Embrace the journey to reach your potential and become the best version of yourself. *Move Forward* is the action of identifying and making progress continuously.

> **"We are designed to succeed and programmed to fail"**
> —Priya Chidanandan

We are programmed to seek behaviors and outcomes that provide immediate gratification, and movement delivers this flawlessly. As you will discover, moving your body strategically and identifying your progress are keys to your journey.

As a movement expert and wellness coach, I'm in a unique position to provide you with applied strategies that work. The concept of personalization means that everything fits as long as it is safe, is body-friendly, and includes progress in ways that are meaningful to you. This book provides the framework and the strategies we recommend for people looking for optimal health and graceful aging. I reference many experts in human behavior, neurology, nutrition, movement, and motivation to help us make these recommendations.

An excellent place to begin your journey is to identify who you are, your authentic self. Your identity dictates behaviors that create the habits and rituals that form your life. What are you passionate about? What is your purpose in life? What fulfills you? This journey helps you unearth these questions.

> **"Outcomes are about what you get, processes are about what you do, and identity is about what you believe"** —James Clear, **Atomic Habits**

I can vividly recall how certain experiences from my childhood shaped my identity, mindset, and behaviors for years to come. These experiences all revolved around movement and work ethic. As early as first grade, I broke through clenched hands in Red Rover, whacked soccer balls overhead in kickball, and avoided others in tag. Little did I know then, my identity would revolve around movement, effort, and the societal expectation to be a provider. For many years, I thought this achievement-oriented mindset and identity was positive in every way.

Unfortunately, it was not. The unraveling process revealed my true self and enabled me to move closer to my potential.

> *"Many of us push towards goals that are not personally meaningful. Slow down, practice mindfulness, non-attachment, and emphasize being over doing. Your health, your well-being, and your authenticity are more important than any job, any promotion, any salary, any degree, or frankly, anyone else's opinion of you. When we get this, when we truly embody it and start living it, then we really can begin to achieve more by doing less." — Dr. Bethany Butzer, a researcher in the fields of positive psychology and transpersonal psychology*

This concept of "less" resonates with me, as I reflexively tend to speed life up and try to work harder and harder (which isn't productive). Like a car stuck in the sand, as I go faster, I am simply getting stuck deeper. I once attended a seminar from Changemaker Nation led by life strategist Lorin Beller. Lorin helped me identify my intention for the year—"Dance with Slow Growth"—to focus my efforts, lighten up, and maximize my potential.

Who are you and what is your intention?

MOVE FORWARD: A MINDSET

Move Forward and reach your potential! Becoming the best version of yourself is something most people aspire to, but few achieve. Reaching your potential is a complex and never-ending process. What if we had a blueprint that you could see and a step-by-step system that you could follow to help you find your way?

My identity drove my behavior for many years. My work ethic became the superpower behind my success, as well as the root of my failures. The effort I put forth was relentless while building a business or finishing a home project. As an early riser, it isn't uncommon for me to wake up at three or four o'clock in the morning to tackle items on my to-do list. The downside of this work ethic, combined with the belief that I must provide and be financially stable, resulted in a failed marriage. My inability to recognize who I was and allow my superpower to run wild with my perceived purpose resulted in an emotional void.

Let's return to that moment I hit rock bottom. I was standing in my new apartment at thirty-eight years of age. My now-ex-wife had cheated on me with a massage therapist we employed in our fitness center. She had alienated my son from me and had requested a restraining order through the local court system.

For the ten years prior, I had supported a stay-at-home wife, had grown a successful business from nothing, had been the best father I could be, and had believed that hard work and providing for my family was the key to success and happiness.

I was wrong—way wrong!

My identity as a provider and a hard worker eroded one of the main pillars of happiness: relationships. According to Dr. German Garcia-Fresco in his book, *Train Your Brain for Success*, there are three pillars in life that lead to happiness: health, wealth, and relationships. If any of these three pillars erode, your ability to achieve happiness flees.

In fact, in one of the longest-running studies on happiness called the Harvard Study of Adult Development, it was determined that good relationships keep us happier and healthier.

> *"We have learned three big lessons about relationships. The first is that social connections are really good for us and that loneliness kills. It turns out that people who are more socially connected to family, to friends, to the community are happier, they are physically healthier, and they live longer than people who are less well connected. The experience of loneliness turns out to be toxic. People who are more isolated than they want to be from others find that they are less happy, their health declines earlier in mid-life, their brain functioning deteriorates sooner, and they live shorter lives than people who are not lonely. The second big lesson we learned is that the quality of those relationships matters.*
>
> *Living in the midst of good, warm relationships is protective.*
>
> *The third big lesson we learned is that good relationships don't just protect our bodies; they protect our brains. People in good relationships have better memories and, in essence, stay sharper, longer."* —Dr. Walter Waldinger, psychiatrist, professor, researcher, and director of the Harvard Study of Adult Development
>
> *"Man cannot become attached to higher aims and submit to a rule if he sees nothing above him to which he belongs. To free him from all social pressure is to abandon him to himself and demoralize him."* —Émile Durkheim, Suicide: A Study in Sociology

Back to my personal story: Years later, I remarried, opened another business, moved into a new home, and had more children. Unfortunately, a relentless work ethic's misguided pattern continued to persist and even escalate with life stress. As time went by, I spent many hours studying and thinking about life, about purpose, and about who I was.

When I look back on my life, I'd rather *not* be known for business success or helping others lead a healthy lifestyle. Instead, being a loving partner, an engaged father, and an inspiring mentor are preferable. The most memorable parts of my life come from spending time with family, friends, and colleagues. I want to immerse my time and effort into diving as deeply as possible into them emotionally. Enhancing relationships allows me to work on the other pillars, with purpose and passion.

When you answer the question, "Who are you?" you'll struggle, as Arjuna does when speaking to Krishna in the book *The Great Work of Your Life* by one of my mentors, Stephen Cope, the founder and former director of the Kripalu Institute for Extraordinary Living.

There are many resources to help you along this path. The void I experienced within my relationships due to my overwhelming obsession with improving my business represented a turning point in my life to answer the question: "Who am I?" Once I answered this question and identified myself as a loving partner, engaged father, and inspiring mentor, my behavior changed to align with that identity almost reflexively. Instead of acting like a buzzsaw and burning the candle at both ends, I spent time developing meaningful relationships. This shift made my effort to enhance other aspects of my life more methodical. If you are struggling with this, a practical example is to write out your eulogy. You may find that the time you are spending today does not align with what you want others to remember about you in the end.

HEALTH AND MOVEMENT FIRST

For many, the pillar of health is the pillar that erodes initially. Without health, happiness is not possible. Without health, wealth is meaningless. Without health, you have nothing. As Warren Buffett says, "The best investment is the investment in your health." Hopefully, the story of my hopelessness gives you insight into how neglecting one pillar impacts your entire life.

My interpretation of the three pillars of happiness prioritizes health. Just as you should secure your oxygen mask before assisting others on a plane, you must prioritize your health in order to be the best version of yourself for others. Health is the vehicle you'll use to travel through time and make an impact. Failure to prioritize your health effectively renders you useless to engage emotionally with others and leave your mark.

Here's my prioritization flow for the three pillars to happiness: **first: Health (energy and vitality); second: Relationships (emotionally engagement with family, friends, and colleagues); and third: Wealth (fulfillment, purpose, and leaving your mark).** Please notice I do not associate *wealth* with *money*. Financial success alone does not enhance true happiness.

According to the National Center for Health Statistics Data Brief No. 360, February 2020, 42.2 percent of adults are obese or severely obese. The Centers for Disease Control and Prevention projected that by 2030, obesity may exceed 50 percent. These projections did not take into account a global pandemic that wreaked havoc on healthy lifestyles. Our reality is much bleaker than anyone could imagine. Many people struggle with preventable health issues such as diabetes, metabolic disorders, hypertension, high cholesterol, and heart disease.

In 2018, the Department of Health and Human Services, based on the Physical Activity Guidelines Advisory Committee Scientific Report, indicated that 80 percent of the members of our society isn't getting enough exercise for optimal health. Falling short or not exercising means missing out on the vast number of research-based benefits, such as more energy, less pain, improved body performance, and a greater quality of life. I recommend reading *The Miracle Cure*, a 2015 report by the Academy of Medical Royal Colleges, to understand better the benefits of exercise.

When I work with a client whose pillar of health has eroded, they often have a negative identity of who they are and a pessimistic attitude toward health in general and exercise specifically. Reaching your potential, being happy, and leading an extraordinary life begins with movement, affirming your true identity, and making declarations of progress.

Somewhere along the way, our society has lost sight of movement as a solution. Movement is medicine!

> "Muscle is the currency of health" —Sara Gottfried, MD

To most, movement is exercise, exercise means a workout, and a workout requires extreme effort and high intensity. High intensity exercise may actually be counterproductive; it can cause injury and ultimately become a barrier to realizing progress, both physically and psychologically.

Bill was overweight, experiencing back pain, and not moving well when I first met him. He identified himself as an out-of-shape, compulsive eater who lacked the willpower to make a change. At nearly 300 pounds and moving poorly, his behavior mirrored this identity. The first day I worked with Bill, we began breaking through this identity and problematic mindset with movement and central nervous system correctives. After a movement assessment and establishing a baseline, we started a breathing practice that resulted in Bill feeling and moving better. We introduced neurological wake-up drills, and his movement continued to improve. We reflexively engaged the muscles within his midsection using neural resets, and *presto!* His total body movement again enhanced.

Bill walked with more fluidity, stood taller, felt better, had less pain, and even smiled. Bill's identity as someone who moved poorly with pain and no control or willpower was evaporating before my eyes. We were using movement to impact his mind and, ultimately, his identity. Bill's outlook changed, and we sharpened our focus during the connect sessions. We tweaked strategies and optimized behaviors such as sleep, stress, nutrition, strategic movement, and cardiovascular exercise while monitoring his progress. Bill's story gives insight into the acute and continual benefits of strategic movement and why we believe so strongly that movement is the solution to reaching your full potential.

At least as far back as the late 1800s, research has been uncovering mind-body connections. Based on his studies, Dr. William James developed what has become known as the James-Lange Theory of Emotion, which posits that:

> *"Human experience of emotion arises from physiological changes in response to external events. Inspired by evolutionary theory, James's theoretical perspective came to be known as functionalism, which sought causal relationships between internal states and external behaviors."* —Harvard, Department of Psychology

> *"I don't sing because I'm happy; I'm happy because I sing"*
> —Dr. William James

Take notice of the power of moving your body and the mental impact it has on you. When you smile, do you feel better? When you stand tall with good posture, are you more confident? When you hold your hands in prayer, are you more appreciative? When you skip, are you more youthful and playful? When you reach your arms up high, are you more triumphant and proud? Social psychologist and researcher Dr. Amy Cuddy explains that the body and mind are in constant conversation and that the body controls the mind. Dr. Cuddy's research also demonstrates that there is a positive hormonal response when we make these physical and mental role shifts.

In his book *The Power of Habit*, Charles Duhigg describes movement and exercise as a keystone behavior. Keystone behaviors positively impact other behaviors. In this case, eating, sleeping, keeping a positive mindset, and even productive financial behaviors improve when someone exercises.

"If you look at your body, without that everything else is out the door. You don't want to be the richest man in the graveyard. If there is energy and vitality, if there is strength, it will show up in your relationships, your business, it's going to show up in your life. That's something you got to master. You can't dabble. It's too important." —Tony Robbins

Speaking of business, progressive leaders understand the bottom-line benefits of being fit personally, and they realize a team that is fit, healthy, and well is more productive and engaged. When leaders embrace wellness and promote the message of "We care about your health and well-being," the work culture improves. Every organization that seeks success and longevity makes wellness a significant component within its strategic plan. Organizations that embrace wellness win!

Wellness takes place within a community and is a collection of behaviors. Wellness includes sleep, stress, nutrition, strategic movement, and cardiovascular training. Optimized behaviors lead to enhanced human cognitive and physical productivity, optimal health, and a higher quality of life.

IS THIS YOUR CALL TO ACTION?

How do you know if your health pillar is eroding?

There are many signs you're failing in this critical aspect of your life. Here is a short list to help you identify whether or not you should Move Forward:

- You lead a sedentary life.
- You exercise sporadically without much structure or rationale.
- Your Body Mass Index is greater than 28 (overweight, obese, or morbidly obese).
- You have a metabolic syndrome (type 2 diabetes, heart disease, high blood pressure, excess body fat, high blood sugar).
- Your body movement is insufficient, as determined by a Functional Movement Screen.

Examples include:
- Poor posture.
- Inability to touch your toes.
- Unstable single leg balance.
- Lack of hip/core sequencing, as demonstrated by an Active Straight Leg Raise assessment.
- Non-proficient squat mechanics.
- Anxiety, depression, or other mental health disorders.
- A need for greater strength, shape, and tone.
- A lack of confidence and energy; you fatigue easily throughout the day.
- Lower back pain or upper back tension due to core weakness, poor posture, or muscle imbalances.

- No personal accountability to progress from a coach, mentor, or community.

If you identify with any of these characteristics, it is time to start solidifying your health pillar. Just asI solidified the relationship pillar to move toward my fullest potential, the time is NOW for you tosolidify your health pillar. Thankfully, there is a path to experience extraordinary living.

MOVE FORWARD: A MECHANISM FOR EXTRAORDINARY LIVING

"He who conquers others is strong. He who conquers himself is mighty." —Lao Tzu

Let's begin understanding Move Forward using the hero's journey around the 21BOOM icon.

Similar to **"The Hero's Journey,"** popularized by Joseph Campbell, think of **"Move Forward"** as the most fantastic superhero story ever told. You will confront the villains within you and overcome the challenges in your path in order to lead an extraordinary life. In its basic form, "The Hero's Journey" follows the archetype called "The Hero" on a journey to achieve great deeds. We all know the story of Superman. Superman follows the hero's journey.

Current State

Superman was born on the planet Krypton as Kal-El, and he was rocketed to Earth to escape Krypton's disastrous doom. He was discovered in a small town in Kansas by a couple and raised to be Clark Kent.

Call To Action

When Clark Kent is about the age of eighteen, he hears a psychic call from the barn where his "parents" have stored his ship. In the remains of his ship, he discovers a glowing green crystal. This discovery prompts him venture to the Arctic to build his fortress of solitude, where he learns that he is, in fact, Superman.

Meet Your Mentor and Embrace the System

Clark Kent receives supernatural aid from his father's crystal, which allows him to build his fortress of solitude, the place where he learns who he is and what he is supposed to do.

Crossing the Threshold

Clark Kent crosses the threshold when he leaves the fortress of solitude as Superman. He reenters society as a new person who must protect the world from evil.

Face Challenges and Confront Villains

There are many challenges for Clark Kent and Superman. First, Clark Kent must impress Lois Lane, acting normal and not giving away his true identity. As Superman, he must save multiple people at the same time. One of the few times he fails is when Lex Luthor launches two missiles, one toward New Jersey and one toward the San Andreas fault in California. Superman manages to save the one headed toward New Jersey, but he fails to rescue Lois Lane from death. However, he does go into outer space and manages to turn the Earth in the opposite direction, rewinding time and saving Lois Lane and California, while also putting Lex Luthor and his partner, Otis, in jail.

Understand Setbacks and Develop Strategies

For now, Superman lives free of the fear that another supervillain will come and try to destroy the world. He lives as Clark Kent and turns into Superman whenever there is the law and good citizens who need protection.

Eventually, when Clark Kent turns into Superman and saves Lois Lane from falling out of a helicopter, he reveals himself to the public. From this point, there is no turning back.

Overcome Challenges

Superman, almost dying because he faces Kryptonite, can be considered the Apotheosis, because Superman never really dies or has a moment of weakness—until he receives the Kryptonite. Superman needs Luthor's girlfriend, Eve Teschmacher, to take off the Kryptonite necklace, thus saving him.

Receive Rewards

This action enables him to finally stop the two missiles from hitting New Jersey and California, save Lois Lane, and develop a relationship with her, as she is the love of his life.

Personal Resurrection and Impact Others

There is no going back to being a regular person for Clark Kent. He chooses to become a protector of Planet Earth. He could've chosen to be evil and take over the world, but he doesn't. Instead, he shows heroism by protecting good from evil while not asking for anything in return. He doesn't expect anything from anyone. His purpose is to protect Earth while enforcing truth and justice for all.

> *"What makes Superman a hero is not that he has power, but that he has the wisdom and the maturity to use the power wisely."* —Christopher Reeve

As in Superman's story, all the points on the Hero's Journey are represented in Move Forward. Take a look at the 21BOOM icon and the integration of this Journey.

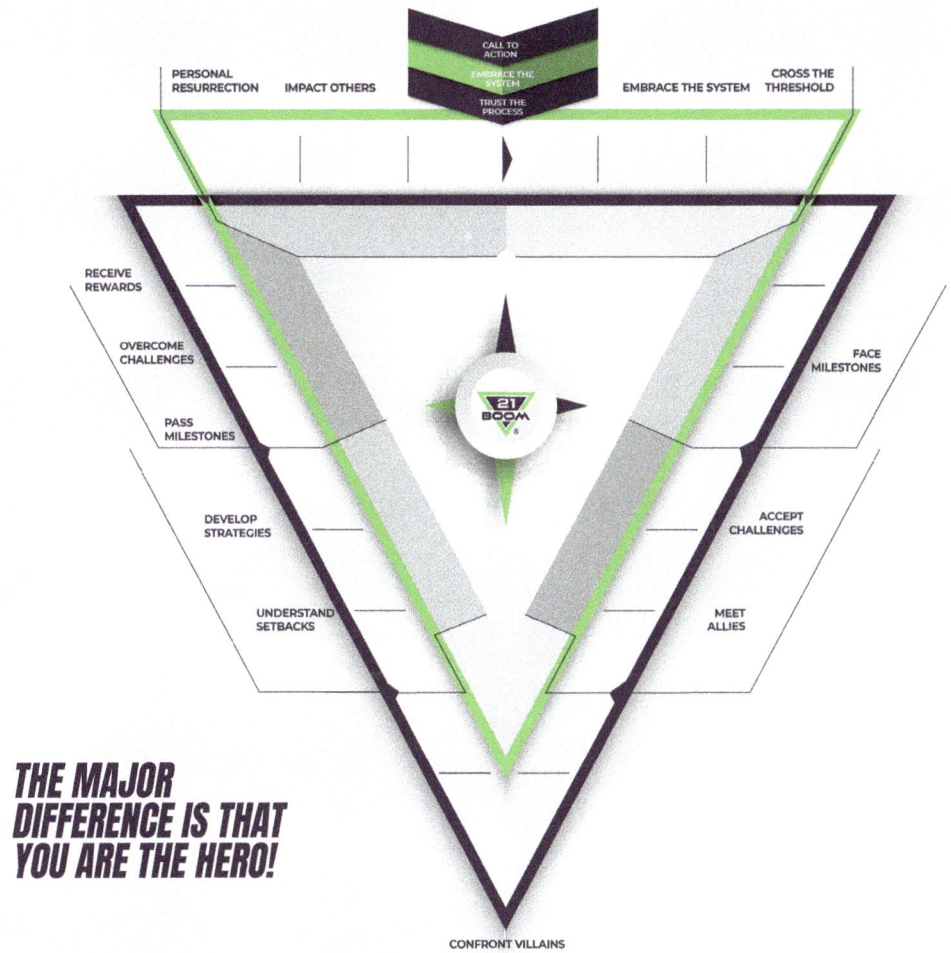

THE MAJOR DIFFERENCE IS THAT YOU ARE THE HERO!

Current State

Your current state is your ordinary world of low energy, self-doubt, discomfort and pain, misguided identity, and potential despair. This stage is a complete contrast to the special world into which you will later venture.

Call to Action

You receive some form of information that shakes up the situation and acts as your call to action. This prompt to leave your ordinary world behind elicits doubt and second-guessing. However, eventually, you realize there is no choice but to Move Forward.

Meet Your Coach

You meet your primary coach, guide, or some form of magical helper, who offers you guidance, knowledge, confidence, advice, and such that will help you on your journey.

Embrace the System

The guidance from your primary coach includes participating in a system that seems reasonable and logical. Based upon your previous experience and current state, embracing the system seems second nature to you, but with a trace of intrigue.

Cross the Threshold

As you set out on your journey, you begin to experience small changes instantaneously. We refer to these changes as progress. You begin feeling better and moving better, and your confidence begins to overshadow the doubt you had before meeting your coach and understanding the system. Every step you make and every aspect of progress you identify takes you further and further along as you cross the threshold between your current state and an unknown world.

Face Milestones

Let the 21 Milestones guide you. These milestones connect and balance the body through a logical somatic transformation system. The science and application of kinesiology, neurology, motivation, nutrition, and human behavior all work together in harmony, delivering body transformation.

Accept Challenges

Every milestone includes a challenge you must overcome. These challenges correct, transform, and ultimately impact both the physiological (hardware) and the psychological (software) aspects of your life.

Meet Your Allies

Along your journey, you'll identify helpers and inner inspirations who keep you going. Typical allies include your primary coach, training partners, significant others, friends, as well as many other allies that lie within you.

Confront Villains

We identify 21 villains that mirror the 21 milestones. Allow me to introduce the 21 villains that are within you:

- Self-doubt (lack of confidence).
- Ignorance (lack of knowledge).
- Body image (negative perception).
- Wrong identity (misguided).
- Ego (delusional).
- Laziness (apathy/indifference).
- Despair (hopelessness).
- Purpose (lack of).
- Fear (uncertainty).
- Envy (comparing yourself to others).
- Sadness (depression).
- Regret (disappointment).
- Anxiety (worry/stress).

- Value (devaluing health)
- Loneliness
- Guilt (remorse)
- Resentment (bitterness)
- Pain (real or perceived)
- Experience (failure)
- Habits (unhealthy)
- Addiction (sugar)

Understand Setbacks

Every great story has drama. You will experience setbacks and failures along the way. Some milestones present with simple solutions, while others take days, weeks, months, and even years to overcome. The key is awareness, acceptance, and making adjustments that help you Move Forward and experience progress.

Develop Strategies

The adjustments you make during your journey are called strategies. Some strategies include increasing cardiovascular training frequency, decreasing the amount of fat you consume, sleeping more each night, tracking your food intake, intermittent fasting, meeting with your primary coach, or eliminating alcohol and sugary drinks. Follow strategies that provide the outcomes you desire.

Pass Milestones

When you identify the milestone in which you find yourself, you build upon the milestone you just passed. It is much like building a house: An architect provides the blueprint, and the contractors then begin erecting the building.

In this case, Move Forward represents the blueprint, and passing each milestone erects the building of your body.

Overcome Challenges

Overcoming each challenge should be celebrated. When you first started your journey, you probably could only crawl for 30 to 60 seconds. As you overcome the 5-minute crawl challenge in Milestone #10 or the 7:30 minute crawl in Milestone #13, the momentum you create begins to impact your mindset.

Receive Rewards

Your journey is perpetually in motion. When you identify progress, you'll become more emotionally connected to what is important and how your body responds to the strategies you employ.

Expected physiological rewards include:

- Greater strength: like Rachel going from zero push-ups to 25 in six months.
- Better movement: like Pawan touching his toes for the first time in his life.
- More stamina: like Jen participating in her first 5k.
- Enhanced functional performance: like Kay being able to walk without a walker.
- Better posture: like Ben going from a greater than 50-degree kyphosis to nearly normal.
- Less pain and discomfort: like Colleen going from herniations, physical therapy, and back pain to being pain-free and highly functional and reaching Milestone #16 in two years.

Expected psychological rewards include:

- Enhanced confidence.
- Greater vitality.
- Lower perceived stress.
- Less irritability.
- More positive mindset.
- Better relationships.
- Greater clarity and mental focus.

Personal Resurrection

When you receive the type of rewards we just listed, you change. The growth you experience both physiologically and psychologically results in a personal resurrection. Your journey through an unknown world has changed you. As you return to a new normal, you think differently, you move differently, you behave differently, and most importantly, you treat others differently. Compare yourself today with the person you were when you began in your current state. Identify how your life has changed.

Impact Others

"Success without fulfillment is the ultimate failure." —Tony Robbins

The final stage in your journey to extraordinary living is the impact you make on others. When we make an impact on others, our lives become meaningful. Your passion drives meaning and fulfillment. Live an extraordinary life by being a role model and giving back to everyone around you. Live and leave a mark for others, and your eulogy will write itself.

Next, we'll cover the seven zones found within the center of Move Forward. Each zone—beginning with the core, moving through the spine, movement, transformation, performance, peak performance, and ending with extraordinary living—focuses and transforms the human body logically.

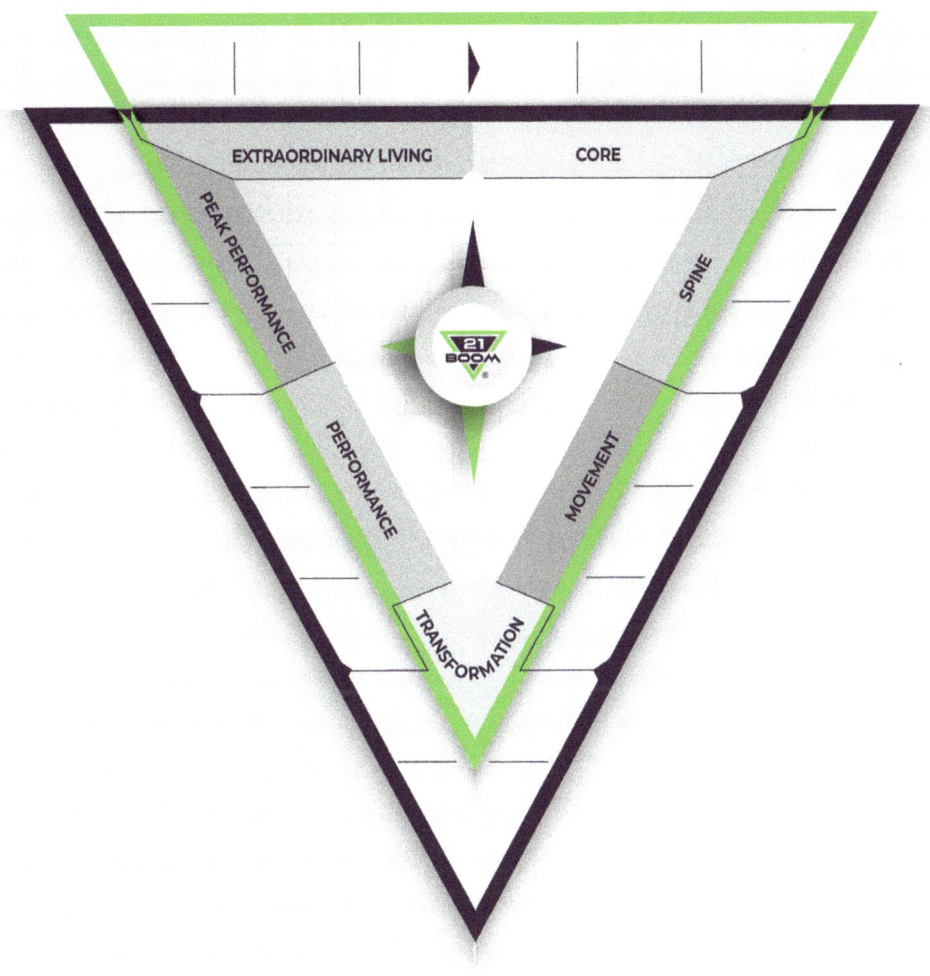

Move Forward Zones include:

CORE

The core is ground zero for movement. Proving proficiency of the reflexive hip/core sequencing found within Milestones #1, #2, and #3 is critical.

SPINE

Once the core is proficient, we focus on solidifying all aspects of the spine in Milestones #4, #5, and #6. Neutral spine, core stability, shoulder mobility, and thoracic rotation all play vital roles in your overall health and function.

MOVEMENT

Now that the core and spine are functioning proficiently, we begin connecting your body from head to toe, utilizing human movement patterns. In this case, the squat becomes the signature movement that ties everything together in Milestones #7, #8, and #9. Squat proficiency opens the door to transformation.

TRANSFORMATION

When your body is functioning proficiently, the transformation process begins. Establish a crawling benchmark in Milestone #10. Dive into learning and practicing special exercises, called kettlebell skills, in Milestone #11. A kettlebell is a tool that conforms to the body's natural movement. When exercises conform to your natural movement, you leverage safety and increase effectiveness. Through kettlebell skills and appropriate load, natural movement patterns begin to transform your body, as objectively measured with a body composition challenge in Milestone #12.

PERFORMANCE

Your baseline health and fitness levels propel growth in strength, endurance, and overall capacity in Milestone #13 (more crawling). You begin to develop injury resiliency with consistency as you explore new double kettlebell skills in Milestone #14. When you prove body composition change in Milestone #15, you'll begin experiencing astonishing mindset shifts.

PEAK PERFORMANCE

Peak performance proficiency requires you to focus your efforts on becoming the best version of yourself through disciplined practice and optimized behaviors. Milestone #16, the 10:00 crawl, and Milestone #17, the modified snatch test, represent formidable challenges on your way to extraordinary living. Once again, you'll prove body transformation with another body composition change in Milestone #18.

EXTRAORDINARY LIVING

The final zone includes the ongoing challenges in Milestones #19, #20, and #21. Every year, you'll perform a 10:00 crawl, pass the snatch test, and verbalize a life goal. Our community gathers online and in person for this annual special event, which we call Move Forward.

Finally, let's focus our attention on the milestones and challenges within Move Forward. The process is simple: move from one milestone to the next by overcoming the challenge associated with each Milestone.

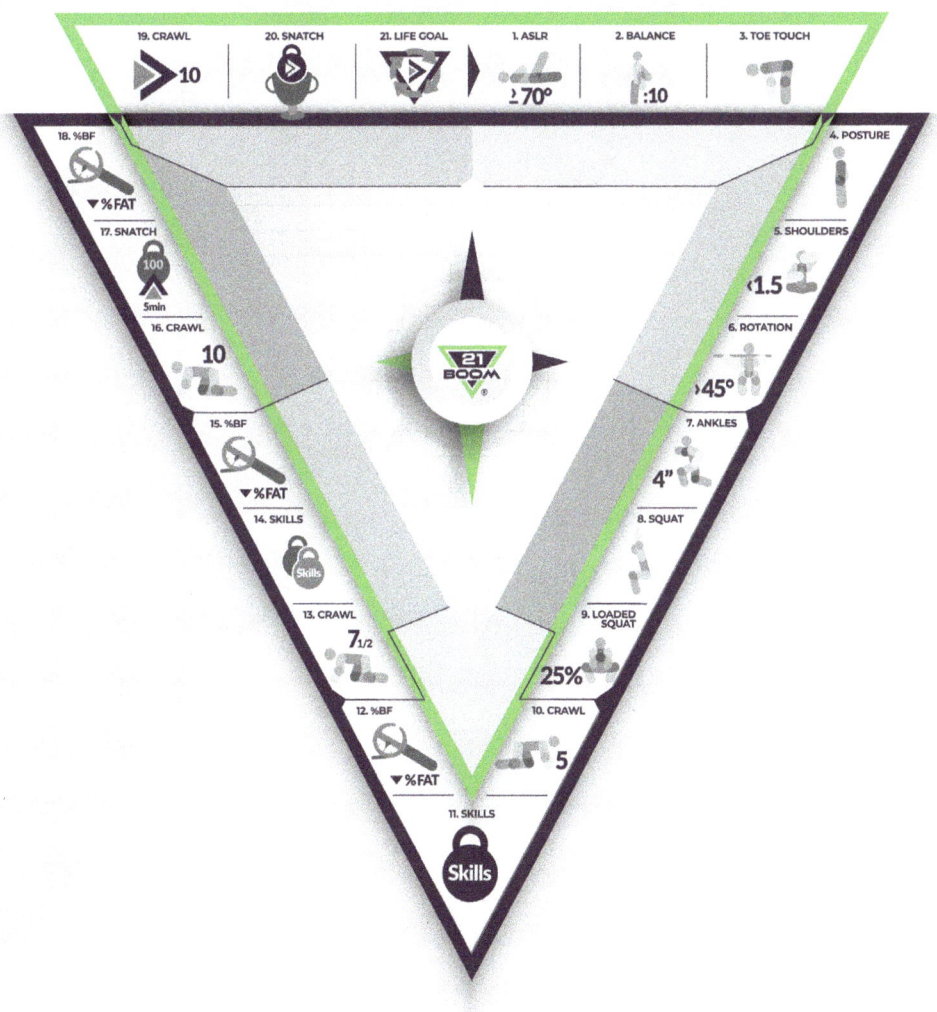

Milestones represent the authentic framework that personalize the movement experience. Move Forward begins by assessing your current state, answering the call to action, meeting your coach, embracing the system, and facing the Milestone #1 challenge. Milestones keep your exercise program safe while transforming your body functionality.

> *Please note: Move Forward challenges are binary. You are either proficient or you are not. You either tackle the challenge or you don't. Many of the initial milestone challenges lean on the movement assessments found within the Functional Movement Screen. You can learn more about these assessments by becoming FMS-certified.*

Milestone #1:

Find Your Flexibility.

ZONE: CORE

The Objective:
Neurally connect the hip/core sequencing necessary for injury resiliency, movement proficiency, and human performance.

The Challenge:
Proficient Active Straight Leg Raise as determined from the Functional Movement Screen Active Straight Leg Assessment.

Proficiency:
Exceed 70° range of motion by the active leg or at least the symmetrical 2 as scored by the Functional Movement Screen (FMS).

Note: In the pictures below and throughout the book, you may notice nail polish on Korey's fingernails. As a father with three young daughters, nail painting is just part of everyday life for Korey.

Proficient

Not Proficient

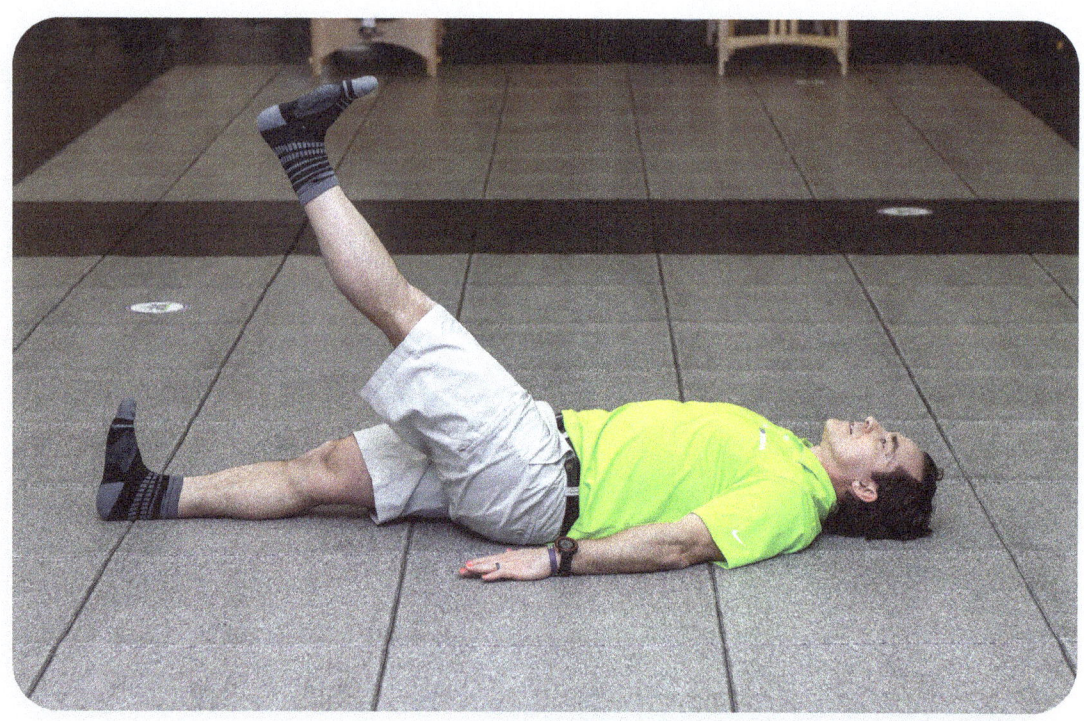

Milestone #1 Challenge Video:

https://vimeo.com/471309280/8b7532f441

Participate in a learn-by-doing seminar for Milestone #1:
https://vimeo.com/648264462

The Outcome:

Milestone #1 proficiency takes you from stiff hips to more mobile hips.

Milestone #2:

Build A Stronger Core.
ZONE: CORE

The Objective:
Improve reflexive core stability necessary for injury resiliency, movement proficiency, and human performance.

The Challenge:
Proficient Single Leg Stance for 10 seconds or Hurdle Step from the Functional Movement Screen.

Proficiency:
Body control is exhibited while standing on a single leg or at least a symmetrical 2 as scored by the Functional Movement Screen (FMS).

Proficient

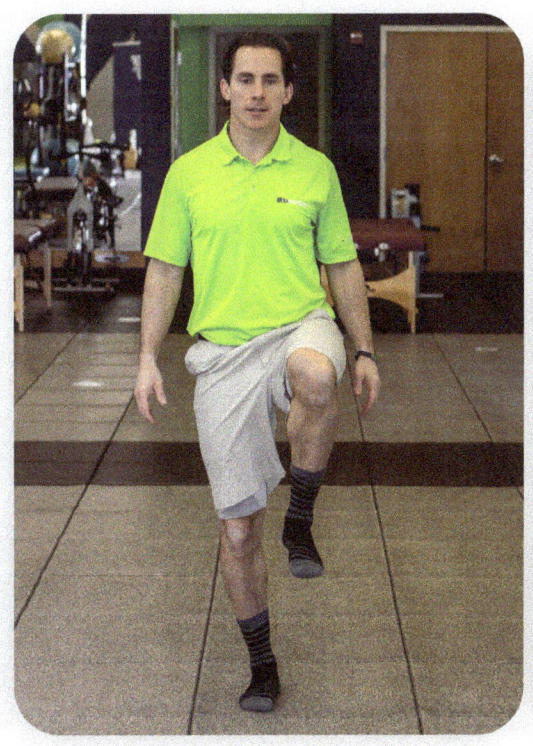

Not Proficient

Milestone #2 Challenge Video:
https://vimeo.com/471329105/2142f71a3c

Participate in a learn-by-doing seminar for Milestone #2:
https://vimeo.com/653395509

The Outcome:
Milestone #2 proficiency takes you from poor balance to better balance.

Milestone #3:

Move Better By Hip Hinging.
ZONE: CORE

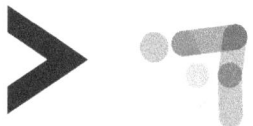

The Objective:
Improve hip/core sequencing necessary for injury resiliency, movement proficiency, and human performance.

The Challenge:
Proficient toe touch with straight or slightly bent knees.

Proficiency:
Successful toe touch from the standing position.

Proficient

Milestone #3 Challenge Video:
https://vimeo.com/471347518/e86b603677

The Outcome:
Milestone #3 proficiency takes you from limited movement to better movement.

_____

Milestone #4:
Improve Your Posture.
ZONE: SPINE

> "We have evidence that the body can shape the mind, and also that role changes can shape the mind." —Amy Cuddy

The Objective:
Improve posture to reduce pain and tension, enhance movement, and transform the mindset.

The Challenge:
Exhibit neutral spine routinely as determined by visual assessments. Neutral spine alignment is when your pelvis, rib cage, and skull align with each other.

> "Standing tall is the best verbal cue to correct postural deficiency"
> —Dr. Stuart McGill.

The concept of a "neutral spine" was put forth by Yale University researcher and medical professor Manohar Panjabi in "The stabilizing system of the spine, Part I: Function, dysfunction, adaptation, and enhancement," J Spinal Disord, 1992 Dec. 5(4): 383–9. The paper outlines a system for spinal stability based on the maintenance of the spine within a "neutral zone." Provided the spine stays within that zone, the structures in and around the spine are generally safe from injury.

Proficient

Not Proficient

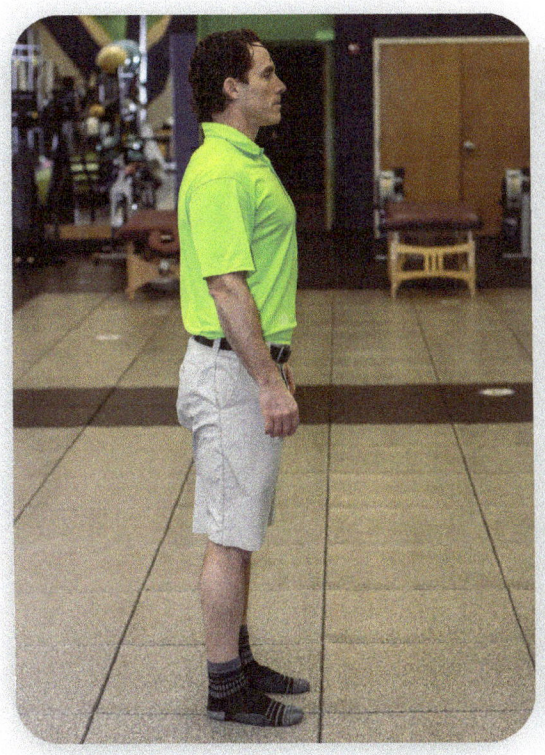 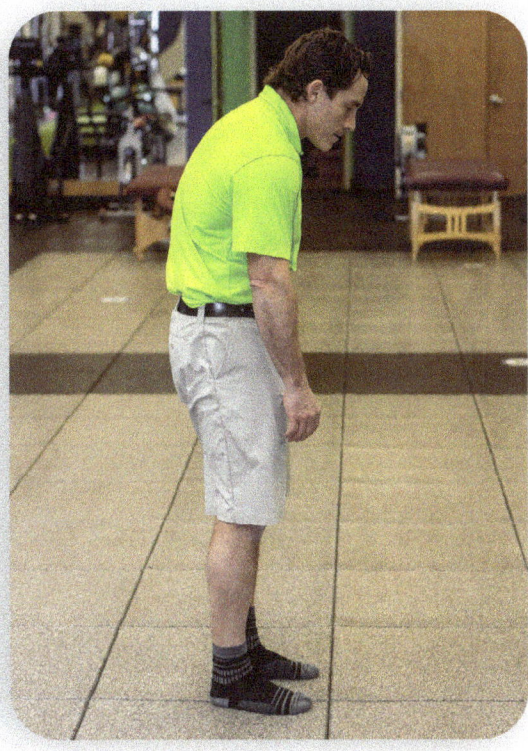

Milestone #4 Challenge Video:

https://vimeo.com/471353871/b63499fd64

The Outcome:

Milestone #4 proficiency takes you from poor posture to improved posture.

Milestone #5:
Find Shoulder Mobility.
ZONE: SPINE

The Objective:
Improve shoulder mobility necessary for injury resiliency, movement proficiency, and human performance.

The Challenge:
Proficient shoulder mobility as determined by a Functional Movement Screen Shoulder Mobility Assessment.

Proficiency:
Less than 1.5 hand lengths between the closed fists with the hands behind the back in an alternating position or at least a symmetrical 2 as scored by the Functional Movement Screen (FMS).

Proficient

Not Proficient

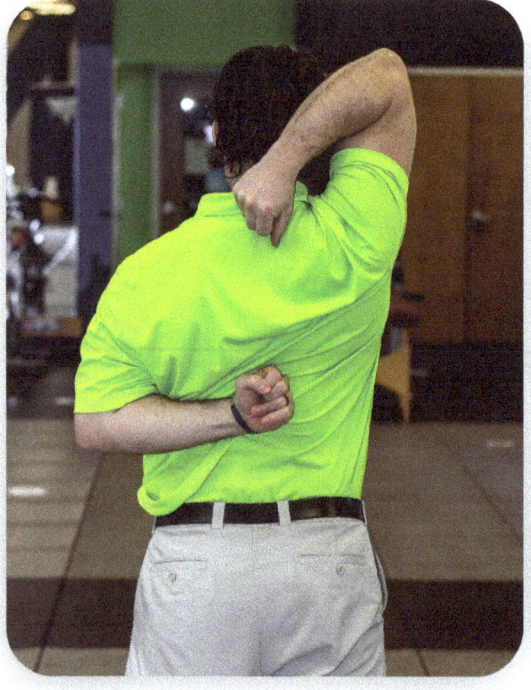
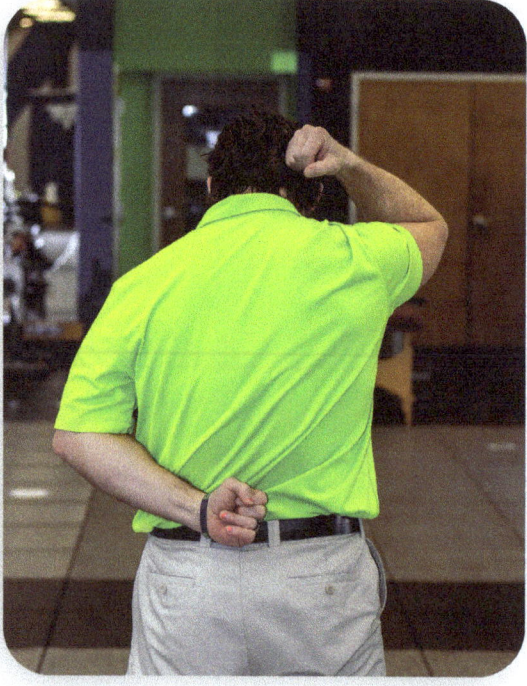

Milestone #5 Challenge Video:
https://vimeo.com/471367276/df43f57e27

The Outcome:
Milestone #5 proficiency takes you from stiff shoulders to more flexible shoulders.

Milestone #6:
Establish Thoracic Rotation.
ZONE: SPINE

The Objective:
Improve thoracic rotation necessary for injury resiliency, movement proficiency, and human performance.

The Challenge:
Proficient thoracic rotation as determined by a Seated Trunk Rotation Test.

Proficiency:
Greater than 45° range of motion while seated with a dowel in front and behind the shoulders.

Proficient

Behind

Not Proficient

Behind
Unable to rotate at least 45 degrees

Proficient

Front

Not Proficient

Front
Unable to rotate at least 45 degrees

Milestone #6 Challenge Video:
https://vimeo.com/471374802/a0eb0c516f

The Outcome:
Milestone #6 proficiency takes you from upper back and neck tension to upper back and neck relief.

Milestone #7:
Improve Mobility From The Ground Up.
ZONE: MOVEMENT

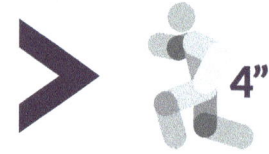

The Objective:
Improve ankle mobility necessary for injury resiliency, movement proficiency, and human performance (specifically squatting).

The Challenge:
Proficient ankle mobility demonstrated through a proficient squat or an ankle mobility assessment. Place a line 4" away from the wall and position one foot with toes precisely at the line. Slowly bring your knee to the wall without lifting the heel.

Proficient:
Exhibited when you successfully touch your knee to the wall without lifting your heel.

Proficient

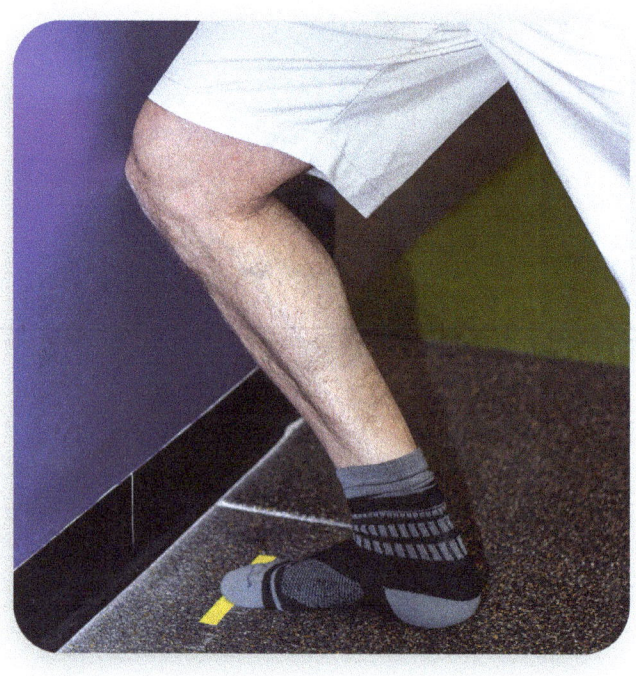

Not Proficient

Knee can't touch the wall with heel down on the ground

Milestone #7 Challenge Video:
https://vimeo.com/471379184/9c191b2e5d

The Outcome:
Milestone #7 proficiency takes you from lower body stiffness to lower body flexibility.

Milestone #8:
Pattern The Squat.
ZONE: MOVEMENT

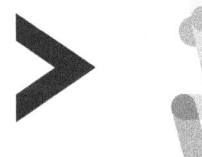

The Objective:
Improve total body movement.

The Challenge:
Proficient squat patterning as determined by a Functional Movement Screen squat assessment.

Proficiency:
Successfully pattern a squat with a dowel overhead or at least a 2 as scored by the Functional Movement Screen (FMS).

Proficient

Not Proficient

Milestone #8 Challenge Video:
https://vimeo.com/471385201/f4d321dade

The Outcome:
Milestone #8 proficiency takes you from poor foot-to-core sequencing to proficient foot-to-core sequencing.

Milestone #9:
Apply The Squat And Connect To Strength.
ZONE: MOVEMENT

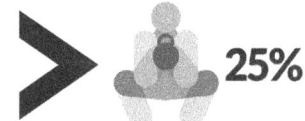

The Objective:
Squat with a load.

The Challenge:
Load the squat with 25% body weight for five repetitions maintaining proficient squat form.

Proficient

Milestone #9 Challenge Video:

https://vimeo.com/471390804/9ecac5bd1c

The Outcome:

Milestone #9 proficiency takes you from squat patterning to loading the squat.

Milestone #10:
Train The Five Human Movements.
ZONE: TRANSFORMATION

The Objective:
Begin following the secret sauce. The secret sauce is the strategic movement found within our Performance Program. This body and mind programming includes six four-week schemes designed to help you feel good, look great, and perform your best. Consistently participate in three strategic movement sessions per week for optimal results.

The Challenge:
Successfully demonstrate a five-minute leopard crawl.

Proficient

Milestone #10 Challenge Video:
https://vimeo.com/471873494/0ce39b40b0

The Outcome:
Milestone #10 proficiency takes you from being unaware of natural movement to moving naturally.

Milestone #11:
Develop Kettlebell Skills.
ZONE: TRANSFORMATION

The Objective:
Learn and practice hard-style single kettlebell skills, including a swing, clean, snatch, deadlift, press, and Turkish get-up.

Follow the secret sauce.

The Challenge:
Successfully demonstrate proficient single kettlebell swings, cleans, snatches, presses, dead lifts, and Turkish get-ups.

Milestone #11 Challenge Video:
https://vimeo.com/471873543/78aefd4b4f

The Outcome:
Milestone #11 proficiency takes you from minimal kettlebell skills to a significant variety of kettlebell skills.

Milestone #12:
Be Consistent To Look and Feel Better.
ZONE: TRANSFORMATION

The Objective:
Pay special attention to eating clean foods and cardiovascular training.

Follow the secret sauce.

The Challenge:
Successfully change your body composition by lowering your body fat percentage.

Milestone #12 Challenge Video:
https://vimeo.com/471873594/3cc22e5e13

The Outcome:
Milestone #12 proficiency takes you from your current body composition to improved body composition.

Milestone #13:

Create More Strength and Power.

ZONE: PERFORMANCE

The Objective:
Add time under tension through the leopard crawl.

Follow the secret sauce.

The Challenge:
Successfully demonstrate a 7:30-minute leopard crawl.

Milestone #13 Challenge Video:
https://vimeo.com/622937846/e5ed16f527

The Outcome:
Milestone #13 proficiency takes you from your current strength to stronger all around.

Milestone #14:

Develop Double Kettlebell Skills to Crush Your Workouts.

ZONE: PERFORMANCE

The Objective:
Learn double kettlebell skills.

Follow the secret sauce.

The Challenge:
Successfully demonstrate a five-repetition double kettlebell deadlift, double kettlebell swing, double kettlebell clean, double kettlebell snatch, double kettlebell press, and double kettlebell squat.

Milestone #14 Challenge Video:
https://vimeo.com/622937902/1f8ce150e8

The Outcome:
Milestone #14 proficiency takes you from single kettlebell skills to double kettlebell skills.

Milestone #15:
Confidence Is The Best Payoff.
ZONE: PERFORMANCE

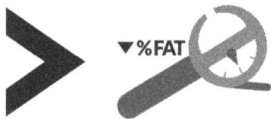

The Objective:
Pay special attention to eating whole and natural foods and cardiovascular training.

Follow the secret sauce.

The Challenge:
Successfully change your body composition by lowering your body fat percentage.

Milestone #15 Challenge Video:
https://vimeo.com/622938439/5d318c08e8

The Outcome:
Milestone #15 proficiency takes you from improved body composition to ideal body composition.

Milestone #16:

Link The Unbreakable Chain.
ZONE: PEAK PERFORMANCE

The Objective:
Add time under tension through the leopard crawl.

Follow the secret sauce.

The Challenge:
Successfully demonstrate a 10-minute leopard crawl.

Milestone #16 Challenge Video:
https://vimeo.com/622938642/e7a885614b

The Outcome:
Milestone #16 proficiency takes you from stronger to more powerful.

Milestone #17:

Activate Peak Performance.
ZONE: PEAK PERFORMANCE

The Objective:
Establish and pass a performance goal.

Follow the secret sauce.

The Challenge:
Successfully pass a StrongFirst protocol 5-minute snatch test using one weight down from your snatch weight kettlebell.

Milestone #17 Challenge Video:

https://vimeo.com/622938691/0a6031a97f

The Outcome:

Milestone #17 proficiency takes you from great workouts to more than just a workout.

STRONGFIRST SNATCH TEST STANDARDS

MALE

WEIGHT	KETTLEBELL	SNATCH TEST
Over 100kg/221lbs	28kg	100/5min
Over 68kg/150lbs and below 100kg/221lbs	24kg	100/5min
Up to 68kg/150lbs	20kg	100/5min
(50-64 years old)	20kg	100/5min
(65+ years old)	20kg	50/3min

FEMALE

WEIGHT	KETTLEBELL	SNATCH TEST
Over 59kg/130lbs	12kg	100/5min
Up to 59kg/130lbs	16kg	100/5min
(50-64 years old)	12kg	100/5min
(65+ years old)	12kg	50/3min

Milestone #18

Looking In The Mirror
Never Looked So Good.
ZONE: PEAK PERFORMANCE

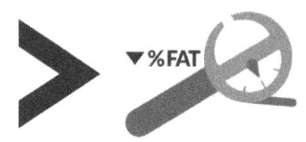

The Objective:
Pay special attention to eating whole and natural foods and cardiovascular training.

Follow the secret sauce.

The Challenge:
Successfully change your body composition by lowering your body fat percentage.

Milestone #18 Challenge Video:
https://vimeo.com/622962392/143df80395

The Outcome:
Milestone #18 proficiency takes you from fit to as fit as you have ever been.

Milestone #19:

Maintain Peak Performance.
ZONE: EXTRAORDINARY LIVING

The Objective:
Participate in a community performance event.

Follow the secret sauce.

The Challenge:
Successfully demonstrate a 10-minute leopard crawl at the annual Move Forward event.

Milestone #19 Challenge Video:
https://vimeo.com/622962176/f35fd714b5

The Outcome:
Milestone #19 proficiency takes you from peak performance to maintaining peak performance and injury resiliency.

Milestone #20:
Live The Active Life And Win.
ZONE: EXTRAORDINARY LIVING

The Objective:
Participate in a community performance event.

Follow the secret sauce.

The Challenge:
Successfully pass a StrongFirst protocol 5-minute snatch test using your snatch weight kettlebell. Every year we hold a Move Forward special event where you can prove to everyone that you can complete 100 single-arm snatch repetitions within 5 minutes.

Milestone #20 Challenge Video:
https://vimeo.com/622937573/82900f1938

The Outcome:
Milestone #20 proficiency takes you from being as fit as you have ever been to achieving the greatest accomplishments of your life.

Milestone #21:
Respect The Practice And The Process.
ZONE: EXTRAORDINARY LIVING

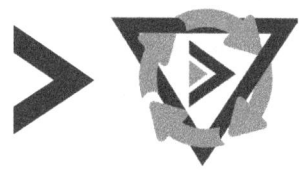

The Objective:
Participate in a community performance event.

Follow the secret sauce.

The Challenge:
Verbalize a life goal to be accomplished by the next Move Forward event.

Milestone #21 Challenge Video:
https://vimeo.com/622937736/d681f75764

The Outcome:
Milestone #21 proficiency takes you from respecting the practice and process to setting an example for others, giving back, and living an extraordinary life.

Here's the hero's journey, zones, and the milestones together.

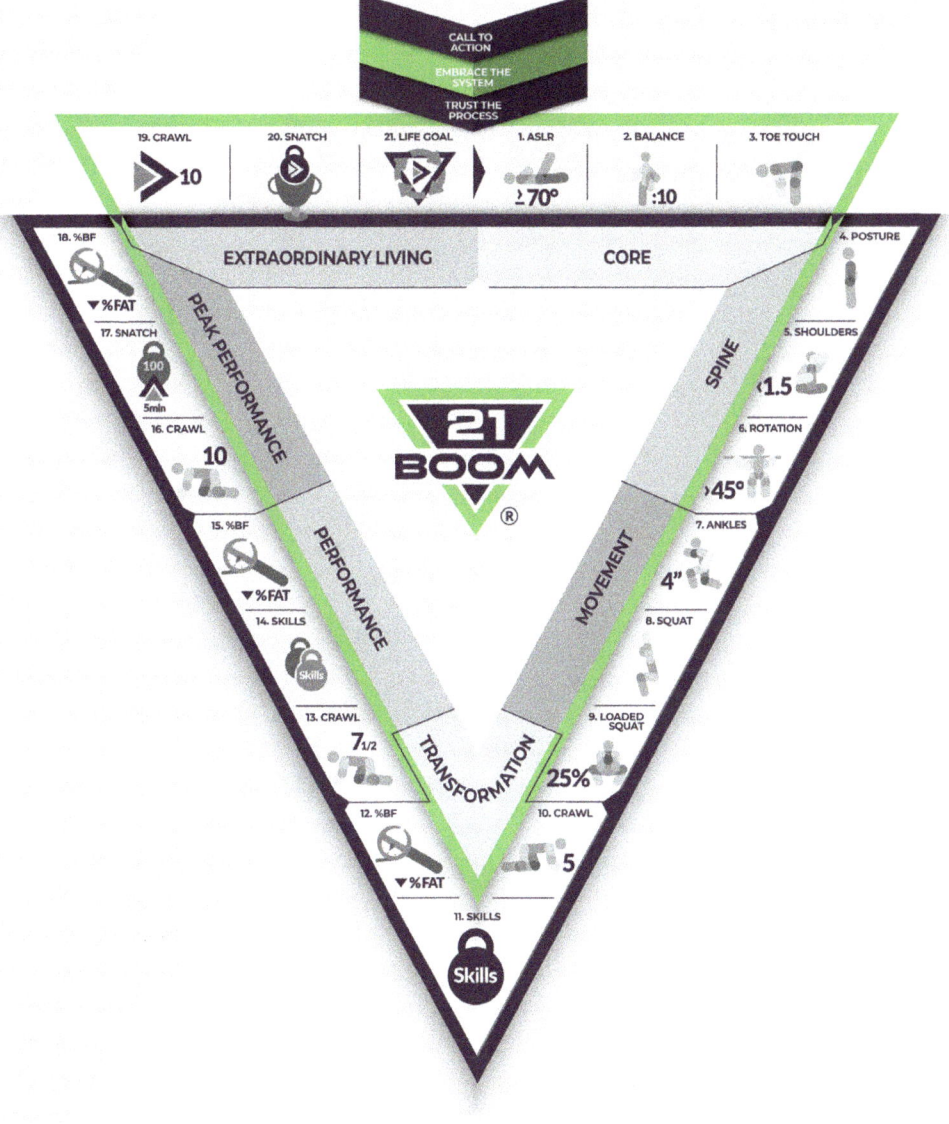

COLLEEN LEONARD CASE STUDY: FROM DEBILITATING PAIN TO PEAK PERFORMANCE

I've laid out how this system will take an ordinary body and condition it to be extraordinary. But what does that look like on a personal level? Beyond the exercises and the strength gained, how does an individual's life change through this process? Let's take a look into exactly what happens when someone experiences Move Forward.

For many years, Colleen was not a very active person. The extent of her daily physical movement was walking and performing her duties as a nurse. In 2010 and in her mid-thirties, she began experiencing periodic back discomfort. Over time, this back discomfort progressed and became more frequent and more intense. She thought this was part of the normal aging process and medicated to manage it. In the summer of

2016, Colleen took a four-hour road trip and was in so much pain that she could barely walk by the time she got out of the car. That was the catalyst that drove her to get a medical checkup to see what was going on.

The diagnosis indicated L4/L5/S1 and S2 herniations, which resulted in a three-month work disability and physical therapy. Medication and physical therapy enabled her to function and get back to work. However, in 2017, the back pain again became debilitating, and she found herself in physical therapy and taking steroid shots and anti-inflammatory medication. After seven long months of this, she realized that finding something that kept her out of physical therapy and back pain would be critical for her quality of life. She stumbled upon our approach to core stability, neutral spine, and human movement at a local health expo in January 2018. During our initial strategy session, Colleen came to grips with how deconditioned her body was when she could not roll over from a lying position. Although Colleen had never joined a gym or wellness program, she decided to meet with us two days per week to work on her health and fitness. Almost immediately, Colleen experienced progress. Her first steps were small. We worked on things like standing tall, engaging deep core muscles, and bringing in the power of breath and neural connectivity. Through these simple actions, her life began to change.

Each milestone presented challenges necessary for Colleen's transformation. She spent weeks and sometimes months within each milestone. The first three milestones that represent the core took many months to solidify. Strategic movements for core stability were routinely executed, with crawling becoming her signature within every session.

Once her core was reflexively stable, we moved into all the milestones associated with her spine.

Posture proved to be a critical milestone to master. We found back pain when Colleen exhibited poor posture. The awareness and mindfulness of Milestone #4: Improve Your Posture became a rallying cry for her training program. For Colleen to ascend the system, she had to exhibit a neutral spine consistently. When friends and family began commenting on her posture, we knew it was time to transition to higher milestones.

With the core and spine strong and functioning, we moved through the next set of human movements with ease: Pushing, pulling, and squatting were mastered in the same measured, safe approach to realistic improvement. However, when it came to tackling the hip hinge, Colleen encountered a challenge, an adversity. Hip hinging and the proper sequencing of her hips and core from an upright position were squarely in the crosshairs of her training program. The setback began as we transitioned from kettlebell grinds to kettlebell ballistic skills. At this point, we took a step back and assessed what we needed to focus on to continue her progress. The corrections needed required fine-tuning tension and posture. With attention on those areas, we were able to deliver breakthroughs in her physiology and exponential growth in her confidence. Colleen successfully passed Milestone #10 with a 5-minute leopard crawl, Milestone #11 with a proficient kettlebell swing, clean, snatch, and Turkish get-up, and Milestone #12 with a reduction in her body fat percentage. She began transforming her body.

Along the way, the identification of progress motivated Colleen to continue. This progress included feeling better, having more energy, experiencing freedom from pain, using heavier loads, learning new skills, and enjoying being part of a community of like-minded training partners.

Following the successful completion of double kettlebell skills, a 7:30 crawl, and improvement to her body composition, Colleen began expressing the type of confidence we could only describe as unbelievable. In the interview to capture this story, she said she thought she was "indestructible." I was astonished to hear the tidal wave of confidence she had acquired during her two-year journey.

At the time of this writing, Colleen is in Milestone #17, and she completed a 40-minute leopard crawl for her fortieth birthday. The peak of our operating system is now within sight. Colleen is proof that anyone can follow Move Forward for optimal health, graceful aging, and extraordinary living and progress from debilitating back pain to peak performance.

This journey was not fast, and it was not easy. But it was successful and empowering. And it has become a cornerstone of Colleen's life, which is the key to any long-lasting behavioral change.

Watch Colleen's entire October 2020 interview here: https://vimeo.com/461365953/1b8105a33c

FIVE LIFESTYLE BEHAVIORS TO OPTIMIZE

There are five lifestyle behaviors you'll want to optimize to Move Forward. They are sleep, stress, nutrition, strategic movement, and cardiovascular exercise. These behaviors work together to maximize health and proper human function. It can be easy to get caught up in buzzwords when it comes to the dizzying world of fitness today. Let's break down exactly how we use these concepts in the program to deliver phenomenal results.

Ironically, the evolution of exercise science is not exercise, movement, physiology, anatomy, or biomechanics. The evolution of exercise science is a person's mindset. It has taken me thirty years within the fitness industry to finally realize the power of the mind: the thoughts we have, the words we say to ourselves, and its associated impact on movement and outcomes.

Our brains are wired in ways that respond to these thoughts and words. Cultivating the Move Forward mindset brings the behaviors

together and propels every client toward personal growth and happiness.

Sleep

Sleep deprivation is considered a form of torture by Amnesty International. Even small amounts of sleep deprivation impair primary physiological and psychological functions. Reaching your potential requires your body to be recharged and firing on all cylinders. High-quality sleep is the starting point for anyone looking to Move Forward.

Review the National Sleep Foundation's recommendations for nightly sleep:

Age Range		Recommended Hours of sleep
Newborn	0-3 months old	14-17 hours
Infant	4-11 months old	12-15 hours
Toddler	1-2 years old	11-14 hours
Preschool	3-5 years old	10-13 hours
School-age	6-13 years old	9-11 hours
Teen	14-17 years old	8-10 hours
Young Adult	18-25 years old	7-9 hours
Adult	26-64 years old	7-9 hours
Older Adult	65 or more years old	7-8 hours

Our recommendations for improving sleep quality include:

- Establish a consistent sleep time.
- Begin an evening ritual that includes a technology detox and meditation.
- Reduce and eliminate bright screens and technology before sleeping.
- Set a cooler room temperature, somewhere around 65° to 68°.
- Reduce and eliminate noise and other auditory distractions.

Are you looking to take a deeper dive into understanding sleep? Try reading the book Sleep Smarter by Shawn Stevenson. Sleep Smarter is a quick and easy read, packed with facts, studies, and scientific insight about getting better-quality sleep. Another option is using a sleep monitor on a smart fitness watch. These vary in sensitivity but will help you monitor the phases of your sleep each night and give you a tool to track your progress.

Stress

> "You can use movement to liberate emotion and stress." —Chris Scott, advanced bodyworker and nervous system specialist

All of us experience stress in our lives.

> "Stress is not only normal; it is beneficial." —Kelly McGonigal, health psychologist

As a coach and movement expert, I view how we perceive stress as the most critical roadblock to overcome. Unmanaged chronic stress wreaks havoc on the body in many ways, including the tightening of arteries, breathing abnormalities, deeply rooted muscle tension, poor posture, movement deficiency, pain, suppression of the immune system, irritability, and food cravings.

Several quick ways to determine if stress is a problem is to complete a functional movement screen or subjectively assess your stress level on a 1–10 scale (1 being low and 10 being high). If you move poorly or subjectively rate your stress as a 6 or higher, we highly recommend that you shift your mindset and establish habits and rituals that help you manage your life stress.

> "Uncontrollable and long-term stress can cause inflammation. Chronic inflammation is related to heart disease, cancer, diabetes, asthma, colds, flu, and major life events." —Melanie Greenburg, in her book Stress Proof the Brain

You must embrace stress for optimal health. Find strategies that work for you. Clients who view stress positively, exercise consistently, have power over their schedules, and practice morning and evening rituals set themselves up to effectively manage life stress.

> "Changing the lens you are looking through and changing your mindset gives you the tools to manage stress. Stop suffering and let go." —Adam Markel in his book Pivot

Just as we do not view a challenge in our physical training as a negative roadblock, we must learn to view mental stress as a similar obstacle we welcome on our journey. When we realize we have the ability to surmount what stands in our way, we are empowered to reach our goals.

> *"It's important to look at the story you are telling yourself. When we are stressed, worried, or faced with uncertainty, we tend to create a story to connect the dots and make sense of it all. The problem lies wherein the story you are telling yourself is one of wishing things were different than they are, because this leads to undue stress. When you can accept the current situation, even though you may be working to improve circumstances, you reduce your stress level and create more of a sense of peace and calm."* —Jennifer Bashant, Ph.D.

We recommend four services for stress relief.

1. STRATEGIC MOVEMENT:

Start moving strategically in either our Performance Program or private training. Strategic movement becomes the most important component of your exercise routine. Following the secret sauce means you'll feel good, look great, and perform your best.

2. GUIDED MEDITATION:

Guided meditation is a process by which one or more participants meditate in response to the guidance provided by a trained practitioner, either in person or via a written text, sound recording, video, or audiovisual media comprising music or verbal instruction, or a combination of both.

3. YOGA AND THAI YOGA ASSISTED STRETCHING:

Thai yoga assisted stretching is a healing art. It is the union of yoga and massage. Receiving Thai yoga assisted stretching is the ultimate way of obtaining all the benefits of yoga, massage, acupressure, energy work, reflexology, meditation, and more without doing it yourself.

4. ADVANCED BODYWORK:

Looking for solutions to unsolved issues? Dive into the intricacies of total body systematic function. Find a nervous system specialist with a background in massage therapy, neurokinetic therapy, restorative breathing, foot therapy, and other somatic therapies.

Nutrition

The old saying *"You can't outrun a bad diet"* is new again in the fitness world, and trainers have universally acknowledged that healthy eating is king when it comes to weight loss. The Move Forward system brings you as far as any physical practice can, in terms of maximizing your fat-burning potential. We do this through developing muscles to burn more calories and utilizing strategic conditioning sequences to create an optimally functioning metabolism. But your eating habits must be examined.

It is essential that you develop a good relationship with food and incorporate strategies that provide the outcomes you desire. You must personalize your nutrition program.

Nutrition Key Points:

- Practice mindfulness and eat only when you are hungry.
- Focus on foods that maintain a normal meal glucose response. High blood glucose levels after a meal alter insulin and promote both hunger and weight gain.
- Reduce sugar intake.

What Is the Best Diet?

> *"We do not have an answer to this question because it is the wrong question. What if differences in our genetics, lifestyle, or good bacteria causes us to respond differently to food? These genetic differences may explain why one diet works for some but not others. The results of our very large data set*

convinced us that responses to food are personal, and diets that maintain normal blood glucose levels must therefore be personally tailored to the individual. They also show, in our view, why the current nutritional paradigm that searches for that one best diet is inherently flawed. The best diet for humans does not exist. Our responses to food are personal, so our dietary advice must also be personal." —Dr. Eran Segal, professor at the Weizmann Institute of Science and researcher in computational and systems biology

Emotional Eating

Nearly every client I've ever worked with exhibits some level of emotional eating. According to emotional eating coach Renee Jones, *"Telling someone who has an emotional eating issue to eat more fruits and vegetables is not an effective strategy. Encouraging them to eat when they are hungry is."* Listening to your body and being more mindful of what your body needs are the most important concepts we teach our clients. If you have a history of disordered eating, we recommend seeing a professional therapist who specializes in eating disorders.

Meal Timing

Eating when you are hungry means you will more than likely not eat every two to three hours. You may not eat breakfast, lunch, and dinner the way you did when you were twenty. Your body may function optimally when you fast for fourteen to sixteen hours per day. This concept, called intermittent fasting, may be worth exploring. Ultimately, it's about finding your way to get there.

> *"The concept of calories in and calories out is not effective. Intermittent fasting is free, fast, and simple."* —Cynthia Thurlow, functional nutritionist

Environment

Amazing things happen when you remove trigger foods from your home. One of the fastest ways to improve your eating habits is to eliminate the foods that cause problems. Typically, these foods are processed and high in sugar. Your environment largely influences your habits. Change your setting to change your practices. In the same way as having your home exercise space ready and laying out your workout clothes helps you stick to your workout routine, preparing your home can help you stick to your good nutrition habits.

Macronutrients

Macronutrients are nutritional compounds that your body needs in significant quantities for daily functioning. The three macronutrients are carbohydrates, proteins, and fats. The historical recommendation to eat higher and higher amounts of carbohydrates may not provide the best outcome. What if this information was tainted by big business to encourage people to consume products that are cheaper to make and last longer on a shelf? Increasing the amount of fat you consume may provide a desirable outcome. Work with your primary coach to find the macronutrient percentage best for you. We encourage you to explore the health benefits of consuming a higher rate of fats in your diet.

> *"Obesity is a hormonal disease. One of the main hormones is insulin. Everything you eat is either a carbohydrate, a protein, or a fat, and they all have a very different effect on glucose and, therefore, insulin levels. When we eat carbohydrates, our glucose and insulin levels are going to spike up fast. When we eat proteins, it looks a lot better. When we eat fat, essentially nothing, a flat line. This is going to end up being very important. Fat is the only macronutrient that keeps our blood glucose low. Fat tastes great and is incredibly satisfying." —Dr. Sarah Hallberg, medical director at Verta Health*

Food Quality

As always, selecting foods that are whole and natural is still a great strategy. Eating 80 percent whole and natural foods may represent an effective strategy to help you move toward your goals. Turning on your genes to do what they are designed to do by eating whole and natural food is the overriding concept in *Nutrigenomics* by Dr. Mark Hyman. Dr. Hyman is the founder and medical director of the Ultrawellness Center.

> *"The most powerful medicine is at the end of your fork, not at the bottom of your pill bottle." –Dr. Mark Hyman*

> *"If it is made by a plant, eat it; if it was made in a plant, don't."*
> —Michael Pollan

Food Tracking

Keeping a diary of the food you consume and analyzing your total calories, macronutrients, and meal timing bring awareness, mindfulness, and accountability. Even if done for short periods, tracking food is an effective strategy for most clients.

Detailed Nutritional Information

The more we focus on nutrients, calories, and the micro details associated with food, the more obese our society becomes. Why do other cultures with less information and research have better health outcomes than we do? It begins with the quality of the food we consume and how we consume it. Shopping for and eating whole and natural foods represents the solution we have moved away from as an industrial society. Personalization is critical; if knowing your total calories or nutrient information helps you move toward your goal, then by all means, use it to help you. "Aha" moments are different for everyone. Nutrition information and strategies resonate when you are ready for them.

What Should You Eat?

Eat foods that maintain a normal blood glucose response and that come in their natural state. If it grows in the ground or is farmed/fished/hunted, you can eat it. Avoid processed foods, foods with more than five ingredients, or things made with ingredients you can't pronounce. If it comes in a box and was made in a factory, avoid it.

What Is a Whole Food?
- Fresh vegetables, such as leafy greens, carrots, avocados, radishes, cucumbers, squash, and sweet potatoes.
- Fresh fruits, such as apples, pears, oranges, watermelon, tomatoes, grapes, and bananas.
- Dairy products without added sugar or chemical flavorings, such as plain Greek yogurt.
- Meat, poultry, or fish that is baked, roasted, grilled, or boiled.
- Legumes, nuts, and products made from them, such as hummus and nut butter without added sugar, unhealthy fats, or chemicals.

What Isn't a Whole Food?
- Anything with too many ingredients, chemical ingredients, or ingredients you can't pronounce.
- Most foods out of a box.
- Most prepared meals in the freezer aisle.

My Favorite TedTalks and Resources on Nutrition
- *What Is the Best Diet for Humans:* https://youtu.be/0z03xkwFbw4
- *Reversing Type II Diabetes:* https://youtu.be/da1vvigy5tQ
- *Lose Weight and Keep It Off:* https://youtu.be/8bE5XLGNPF0
- *The Mathematics of Weight Loss:* https://youtu.be/vuIIsN32WaE
- *Intermittent Fasting:* Transformational Technique: https://youtu.be/A6Dkt7zyImk
- *How to Make Healthy Eating Unbelievably Easy:* https://youtu.be/Q4yUlJV31Rk
- *The Mindset for Healthy Eating:* https://youtu.be/E5TIpQsOAHU
- *That Sugar Film* video documentary

MEAL IDEAS
Here is a 7-Day Low-Carb Meal Plan from Dr. Sarah Hallberg: https://lowcarbaction.org/

Approximate daily nutritional information:

2000 calories

20% protein; 8% carbohydrate; 72% fat

DAY 1

BREAKFAST ▷
Scrambled eggs and Sautéed Spinach

2 eggs, scrambled with 1 oz Monterey Jack cheese, 1 Tbsp butter, and salt
1 cup sautéed spinach in 1 Tbsp olive oil and salt1 cup brewed coffee with 1 Tbsp heavy cream

LUNCH ▷
Cobb Salad

2.5 oz grilled chicken, 1 slice bacon, hard-boiled egg, 1 oz blue cheese, 1/4 avocado, 1/2 cup diced tomatoes over 2.5 cups lettuce (romaine, bibb, and watercress) topped with 2 Tbsp red wine vinaigrette, salt and pepper

DINNER ▷
Beef Stir Fry

3 oz beef sirloin with sautéed vegetables (1/2 cup broccoli, 1/2 cup sweet bell peppers, 2 Tbsp onion, garlic) and 2 Tbsp cashews mixed with 1 Tbsp olive oil, 2 Tbsp soy sauce, vinegar, and salt

SNACKS ▷
1 oz Macadamia nuts, roasted, salted
1/2 cup strawberries

DAILY NUTRIENT INFORMATION

2027 calories; 99 g protein; 51 g carbohydrate; 165 g fat

DAY 2

BREAKFAST ▸
Cream Cheese Pancakes w/ Almond Butter

Pancakes: 2 eggs, 2 oz cream cheese, cinnamon, vanilla extract made with 1 Tbsp butter and topped with 1 Tbsp almond butter, 1 cup brewed coffee with 1 Tbsp heavy cream

LUNCH ▸
Salmon Kale Caesar Salad

4 oz salmon grilled with 1.5 Tbsp avocado oil over 2 cups romaine lettuce + 1 cup kale, 1/4 avocado, 3 Tbsp shredded parmesan cheese tossed in 2 Tbsp Caesar Dressing and salt

DINNER ▸
Rosemary Pork Chops and Sautéed Green Beans

5 oz boneless pork chop pan-fried in 1 Tbsp olive oil with a side of 1 cup green beans, 2 Tbsp onions, 3 Tbsp slivered almonds sautéed in 1 Tbsp butter and salt
85% dark chocolate square (1/2 oz)

SNACKS ▸
1 cup Bell pepper sticks and 1 Tbsp Ranch dressing

DAILY NUTRIENT INFORMATION

2030 calories; 98 g protein; 49 g carbohydrate; 165 g fat

DAY 3

BREAKFAST ▸
Steak and Eggs with tomato slices

1 oz Flank steak and 2 eggs scrambled in 1 Tbsp butter Tomato slices, salt and pepper
1 cup brewed coffee with 1 Tbsp heavy cream

LUNCH ▸
Ham and Cheese Rollups with Vegetable Sticks

Roll-ups made with 3 oz Ham and 3 oz Provolone cheese, 2 Tbsp Mayonnaise, 1 dill pickle, 1/2 cup cucumbers slices and 1/2 cup carrot sticks 1 cup unsweetened chocolate almond milk

DINNER ▸
Buffalo Wings and a Side Salad

4 oz chicken wings with Buffalo sauce (2 Tbsp butter and 1 Tbsp hot sauce) dipped in 1.5 Tbsp Blue cheese dressing
Side salad – 1.5 cups Mixed greens, 1/4 cup Cheddar cheese, 1 Tbsp flax seeds, and 1 Tbsp Ranch dressing

SNACKS ▸
6 oz Plain, whole milk yogurt and 2 Tbsp flax seeds

DAILY NUTRIENT INFORMATION

2004 calories; 104 g protein; 51 g carbohydrate; 155 g fat

DAY 4

BREAKFAST ▶
Vegetable and Cheese Omelet with Sausage

2 Eggs, 1 oz goat cheese, 3/4 cup spinach, 3/4 cup mushrooms cooked in 1 Tbsp butter, salt and a side of 2 oz pork sausage
1 cup brewed coffee with 1 Tbsp heavy cream

LUNCH ▶
Tuna Salad Lettuce Wraps

3 oz Tuna (chunk light) mixed with 2 Tbsp mayonnaise, 1 Tbsp flax seeds, 1 tbsp dijon mustard, 1/2 cup beets, 1 Tbsp diced celery, 1 Tbsp chopped onion, salt and pepper in Boston bibb lettuce leaves with a side of 1/4 cup brazil nuts

DINNER ▶
Bunless Cheeseburger and Parmesan Brussel Sprouts

3 oz ground beef burger topped with 1 oz gruyere cheese, tomato and onion
Side of 3/4 cup roasted brussel sprouts and 1 oz shredded parmesan tossed in 1.5 Tbsp olive oil with salt

SNACKS ▶
1/4 cup Macadamia nuts, 1 cup unsweetened chocolate almond milk

DAILY NUTRIENT INFORMATION
2017 calories; 105 g protein; 53 g carbohydrate; 159 g fat

DAY 5

BREAKFAST ▶
Ham and Swiss Omelet with Turnip "Home Fries"

Omelet made of 2 Eggs, 2 oz Ham, 1 oz Swiss cheese, 1 Tbsp butter, and salt
Side of 3.4 cup Turnips (cubed) sautéed in 1 Tbsp olive oil, 1 Tbsp scallions, and salt
1 cup brewed coffee with 1 Tbsp heavy cream

LUNCH ▶
Chicken Caesar Salad

3 oz grilled chicken with 1 Tbsp olive oil over 3 cups romaine lettuce, 2 Tbsp shredded parmesan cheese tossed in 2 Tbsp Caesar Dressing, salt, and pepper

DINNER ▶
Tacoless Tacos

3 Boston bibb lettuce leaves with 3.5 oz ground beef mixed with taco seasoning, 1/4 cup bell peppers, 1/4 cup diced tomatoes, 2 Tbsp grilled onions, 1/4 cup Mexican cheese blend, 2 Tbsp sour cream, 3/4 avocado

SNACKS ▶
1/2 cup blueberries, 2 Tbsp flax seeds, 3 Tbsp heavy whipping cream

DAILY NUTRIENT INFORMATION
1988 calories; 103 g protein; 47 g carbohydrate; 158 g fat

DAY 6

BREAKFAST
Yogurt, Almonds, and Raspberries
6 oz plain, whole yogurt, 3 Tbsp heavy cream, 2 Tbsp almonds, 1/2 cup raspberries 1 cup brewed coffee with 1 Tbsp heavy cream

LUNCH
Greek Chicken Salad with Balsamic Vinaigrette
2.5 cups mixed greens and spinach, 4 oz Grilled chicken, 1/4 cup cucumber, 1 oz Goat cheese, 6 olives, 1/2 cup beets, 1/2 avocado, 1/2 cup bell peppers topped with 1.5 Tbsp olive oil, 2 tsp balsamic vinegar, salt and pepper

DINNER
Shrimp Scampi over Zucchini Noodles
5 oz shrimp sautéed in 1.5 Tbsp butter, 1/2 Tbsp olive oil, 1.5 fl oz white wine, 1 garlic clove, parsley, lemon juice, salt and pepper over 1 cup zucchini noodles and 1/2 cup steamed broccoli mixed with 1.5 Tbsp olive oil, salt, and pepper

SNACKS
1 oz cheese and 1 oz pepperoni

DAILY NUTRIENT INFORMATION
1964 calories; 100 g protein; 50 g carbohydrate; 154 g fat

DAY 7

BREAKFAST
Fried Eggs and Sausage over Sautéed Kale
2 eggs fried in 1 Tbsp butter over 1.25 cups kale sautéed in 1.5 Tbsp olive oil and salt with a 2 oz side of sausage
1 cup brewed coffee with 1 Tbsp heavy cream

LUNCH
Roasted Chicken with Dill and Steamed Broccoli
3.5 oz Roasted chicken breast topped with a dill olive oil (1/2 Tbsp) and butter (1/2 Tbsp) blend and a side of 1 cup steamed asparagus, 1/2 Tbsp butter, salt, and pepper

DINNER
Stuffed Peppers
1 large Bell pepper stuff with 4 oz ground beef cooked with 1/2 Tbsp olive oil, 1/4 cup 'riced' cauliflower, 2 Tbsp sautéed onions, 1/4 garlic clove, 1/4 cup mozzarella cheese, 1/4 cup tomato sauce, salt and pepper

SNACKS
3 oz guacamole with 1/2 cup cucumber slices and 6 radishes.
1/4 cup pecans and 1/2 cup strawberry slices, 1 cup unsweetened chocolate almond milk

DAILY NUTRIENT INFORMATION
1975 calories; 100 g protein; 51 g carbohydrate; 157 g fat

Just like physical fitness is a process, mastering your nutrition is also a lifelong journey. Educate yourself on the basics of healthy fat loss and study those who have achieved long-lasting results through a maintainable diet.

MOVEMENT IS THE MAGIC PILL

> "Exercise makes you smarter." —Dr. Peter Blomstrand, clinical physiology researcher

We choose to separate movement into two lifestyle behaviors: strategic movement and cardiovascular training. It is essential to realize the importance of each, as they will bring maximal benefit when done independently. Create structure within your week by scheduling exercise into each day, and then show up! Consistency is the master key.

Time is your most precious nonrenewable asset. We recommend investing 3 percent of your day to movement, which translates into just 43 minutes. Isn't your health worth this small investment?

We follow three central movement concepts:

1. Personalize your training.
2. Include body-friendly movements and science-based programming.
3. Identify progress following each session.

We personalize and optimize movement, which is our specialty. Let's take a deeper dive into the most authentic component of Move Forward: personalized strategic movement through our performance program.

> "Exercise is dose-dependent, so more is not better." —Dr. Barry Franklin and the American Heart Association scientific statement

STRATEGIC MOVEMENT IS THE ANTIAGING ELIXIR

> "Do what is necessary, not what is possible." — Pavel Tsatsouline

When most people think of exercise, they think of cardiovascular exercise. Cardiovascular exercise is important, and we will cover that; however, strength changes everything. If you improve your strength, you get faster; if you improve your strength, you reduce your risk of injury; if you improve your strength, you burn more calories at rest, if you improve your strength, you increase your stamina, if you improve your strength, you change your life. We consider strategic movement to be the antiaging elixir because our body is losing lean muscle mass and the ability to generate power through type II muscle fibers as we age.

We find that people who need strategic movement the most are the least likely to do it.

Walking requires no coaching. Walking is a reflexive and beneficial form of exercise that can and should be done by everyone. Strength training, on the other hand, is a learned skill that must be personalized and practiced. Strength training *requires* professional coaching. There is an order of operation to follow for safe progression. Failure to observe this warning can result in injury, frustration, a problematic mindset, and potentially life-altering medical procedures.

Note the systems and principles we use to deliver personalization and progression. These systems are led by passionate professionals who have devoted their lives to helping others realize their potential.

Each system has its organization, certifications, books, and resources, which we highly recommend. These six systems provide the principles found deep within Move Forward and are listed here in no particular order:

- **Neurosomatic Balancing**

Neurosomatic balancing resolves deeply rooted central nervous system and mindset obstacles that play a role in movement deficiency, pain, performance, goal achievement, and personal growth.

Effective aspects of neurosomatic balancing include the use of sensory awareness and mindfulness. Neurosomatic balancing retrains your brain to change how your body responds to internal and external stressors. This particular form of self-sensing, or sensory awareness, leads to self-regulation that can be used everywhere in daily life to prevent imbalances or reflexive strain patterns from developing. Our bodies are incredibly intelligent, sensitive, and responsive, and they use communication systems that are exceptional. They are scanning and reading our every move—each thought, belief, and intention—with exquisite precision and speed. Consciously participating in this communication system can have remarkable results.

An example of this is lying on your back and connecting your mind and body through "mapping." Lie on your back, close your eyes, and use your mind to outline your entire body slowly. Pay attention to how each area of your body feels. Do your ankles feel tight, does your lower back feel heavy, is your upper back tense? This somatic mapping begins to connect the mind to the body in powerful ways that open the possibility of improved communication, resulting in less discomfort, better movement, and improved living.

- Back-Fit Pro Dr. Stuart McGill

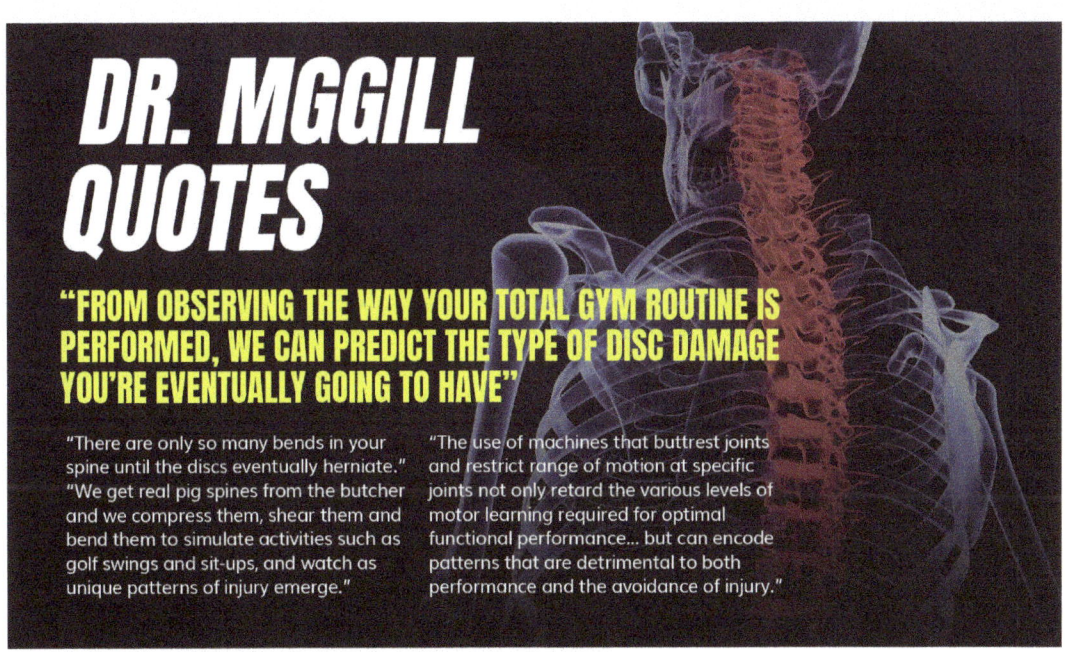

- Functional Movement Systems, Gray Cook and Lee Burton

- Reflexive Performance Resets, Chris Korfist, J.L. Holdsworth, and Cal Dietz

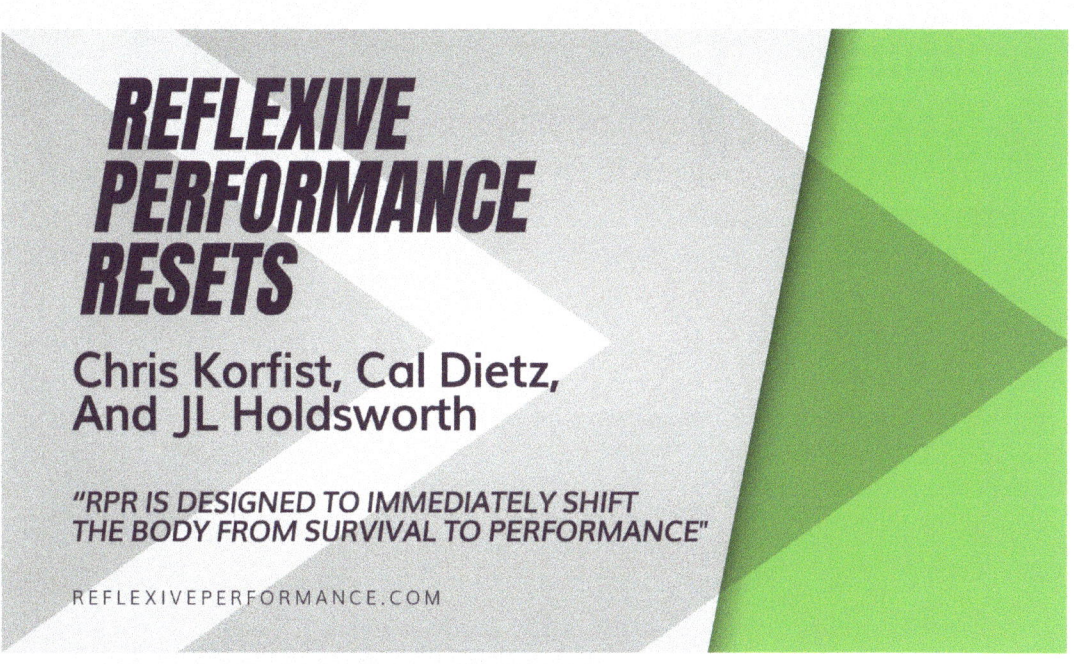

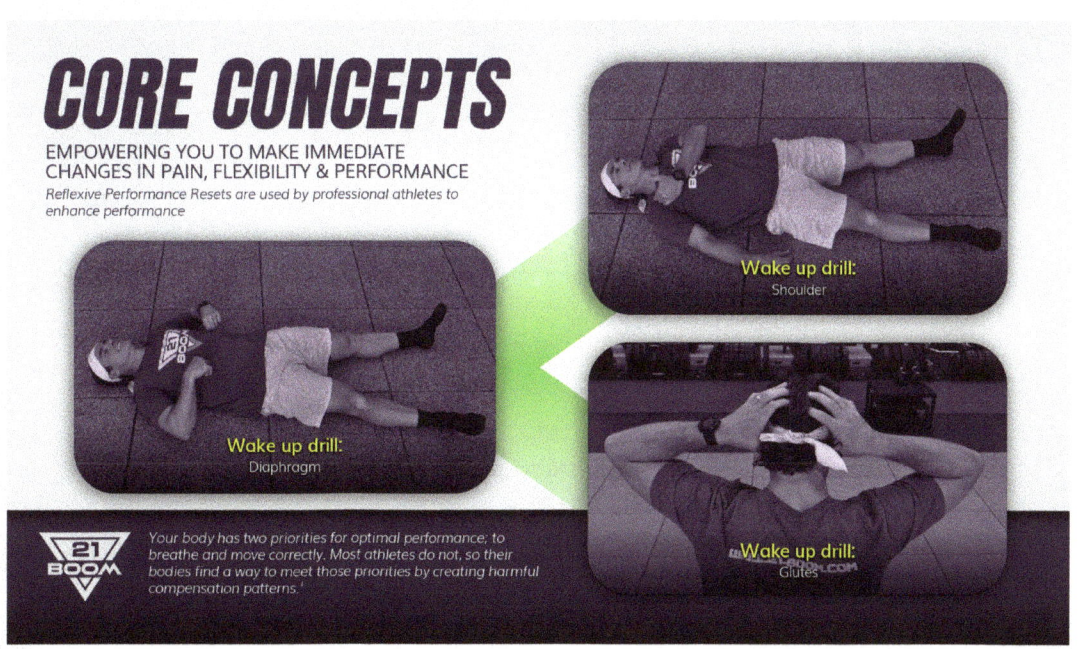

- Original Strength, Tim Anderson

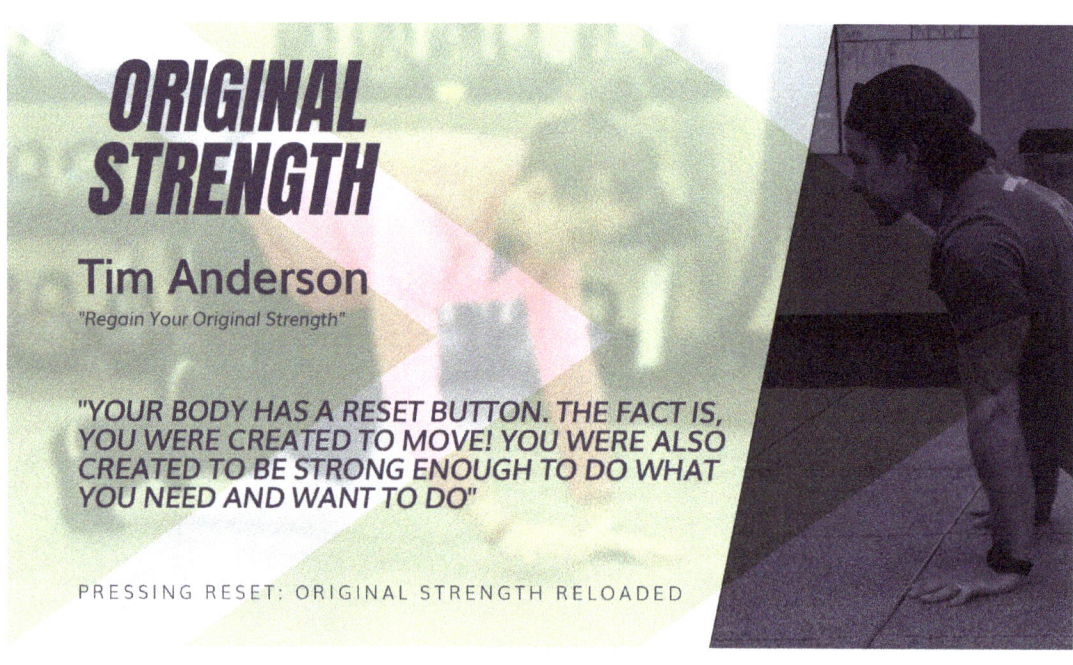

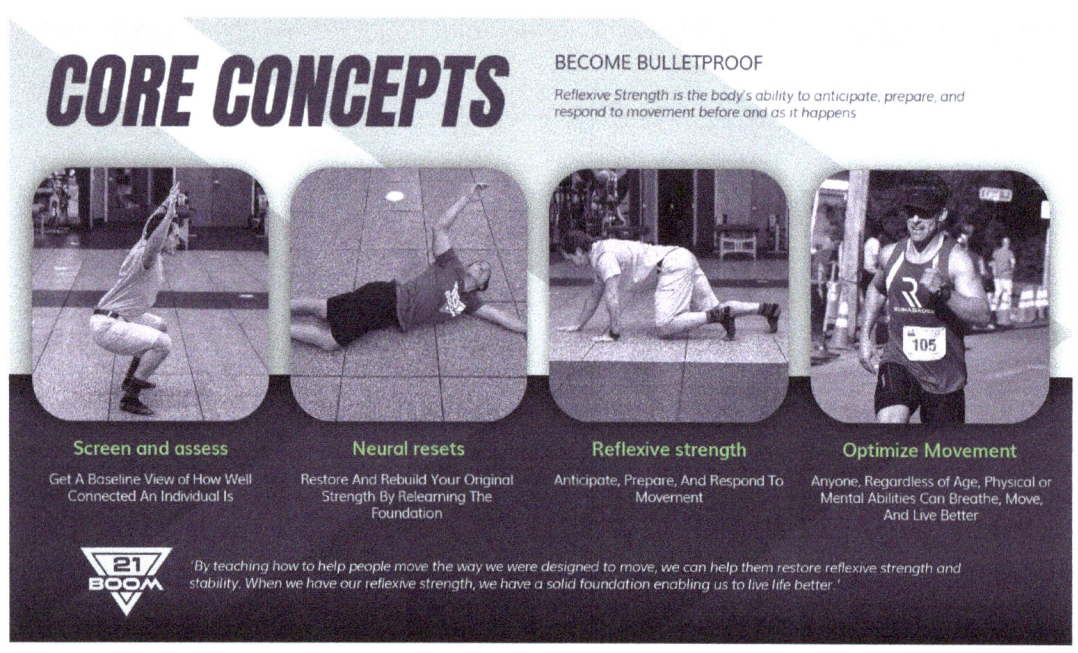

- StrongFirst, Pavel Tsatsouline

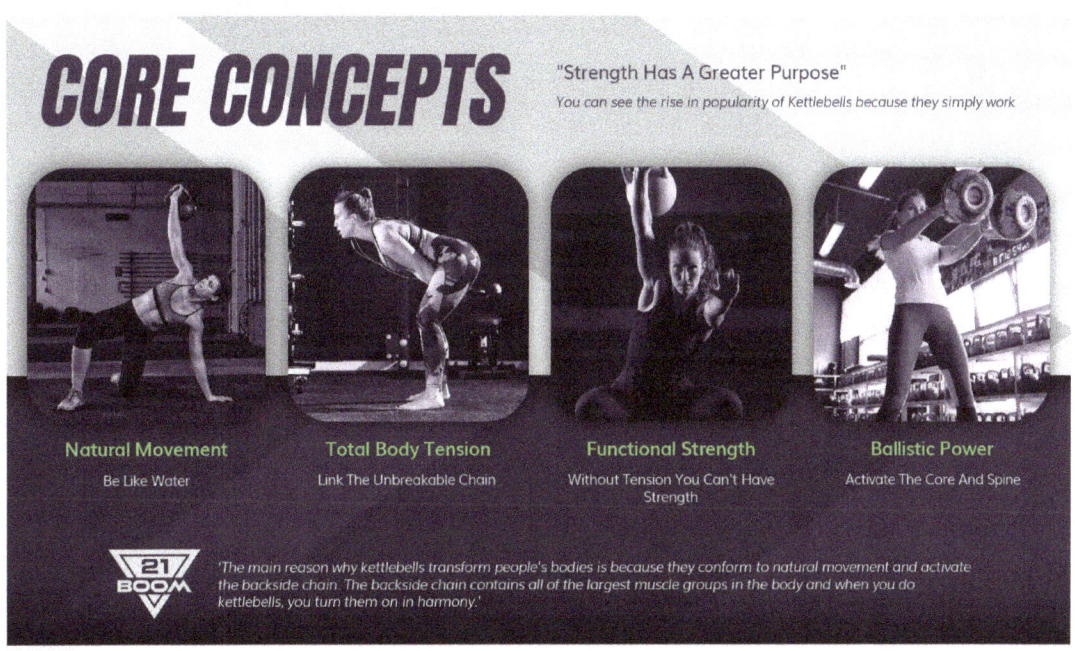

If your idea of strength training is going to a gym and sitting on a circuit of select electrified machines or pumping out a few dumbbell arm curls and chest presses, I have bad news for you. If your strength training idea is jumping into a boot camp and timing random exercises sprinkled with Olympic lifts, I have bad news for you. You see, to keep strength training safe and effective, you must personalize the program and move in a body-friendly way. Whether you are just beginning to strength-train or you have strength-trained for thirty years, start with the Milestone #1 challenge and make sure you are proficient. Move from milestone to milestone with purpose and clarity.

Next, let's provide you with specific movement recommendations for each milestone. Remember, these recommendations represent starting points and educated guesses. You should always follow strategies, movements, and programming that provide the best outcome. Use the assessments for each milestone described previously and work with your primary coach to fine-tune these recommendations.

ASCEND MILESTONES!

STRATEGIC MOVEMENT FOR MILESTONES 1-9

Milestone #1:
Find Your Flexibility.

ZONE: CORE

One-week strategic movement program
Recommended equipment: Cook Band

VIDEO RESOURCES:

Milestone #1 Day 1 and Day 4:
https://vimeo.com/471312510/938a7717c8

Milestone #1 Day 2 and Day 5:
https://vimeo.com/471326005/8b0258d7a7

Milestone #1 Day 3, Day 6, and Day 7:
https://vimeo.com/471327482/767b021cba

Day 1 and Day 4 Strategic Movement Session for Milestone #1:

- **Breath: 1 x :60 - P. 135**

Relaxed position

Exercise Description: Lie on your back with your arms, legs, and head in a relaxed position.

- **Lower body segmental rolling: 3 x 1 full roll each side P. 136-137-138**

Exercise Description: Let's reflexively activate some of the deepest midsection muscles we have. Begin by lying on your back. Lift one leg and bring it across your body. Lift your head and look in the direction you are rolling. Using your midsection muscles, slowly roll to your stomach while leading with the leg. Once on your stomach, lift one leg, look in the direction you are rolling, and bring the leg across your body. Using your midsection muscles, slowly roll to your back.

- **Head nod 1 x 5 side to side - P. 138**

Exercise Description: People who do not move their heads and necks are not well. Let's connect your body through head nods. You can execute head nods in any body position. Lie on your stomach and gaze forward with your chin on an imaginary shelf. Slide your chin on that shelf and bring your gaze behind you, paying attention to the connection between your torso, neck, and head. Repeat for the other side.

- **Hip rock 1 x 5 - P. 139-140**

Exercise Description: Just as you experienced as a baby, we're going to mobilize your hips and connect your body reflexively. Begin in a tabletop position, widen your knees, and sit on your heels. Extend your arms and begin rocking your hips forward. When your hips reach full extension, return to the starting position and repeat.

- **Single leg hip rock 1 x 5 each - P. 140**

Exercise Description: From the hip rock position, extend one leg directly to the side. Rock your hips forward and backward as you feel a stretch of your inner hip musculature.

- **Side to side pigeon pose 1 x 5 - P. 141-142**

Exercise Description: Begin in a tabletop position. Lift your knees and slide one leg up and through so that the outer aspect of the leg is in contact with the floor. You'll experience a glute stretch when you sit the hips down and extend the opposite leg. This is a great time to add another head nod.

- **Active straight leg raise corrective 3 x 10 - P. 143-144**

Exercise Description: Use a Cook Band or resistance band. Lie on your back with legs and arms extended. Bring your hands with the band to your hips. Keeping your legs locked and toes tucked toward your knees, lift one leg as far as you can. Return the leg to the ground and bring your arms back to the starting position.

- **Glute bridge 3 x 10 - P. 145**

Exercise Description: Lie on your back with your knees bent. Lift your hips to full hip extension and return to the ground.

- **Modified side plank 3 x :15 - P. 146**

Exercise Description: Lie on your side with knees bent at 90°. Lift your hips and remain in a neutral spine. Hold for the recommended amount of time. To increase the intensity, extend your legs so your feet become the endpoint and not the knees.

- **Bird dog 2 x 10 - P. 170-171**

Exercise Description: Begin in a tabletop position. Extend one arm and opposite leg fully while maintaining a neutral spine and return extremities to the starting position.

- **Multidirectional marching - P. 147**

Exercise Description: Stand tall. Begin lifting one knee while bringing the opposite arm upward. Return to the starting position and continue this contralateral motion in any direction. Forward, backward, and side-to-side marching all enhance the vestibular system.

Day 2 and Day 5 Strategic Movement Session for Milestone #1:

- **Breath: 1 x :60 - P. 135**

Relaxed position

- **Diaphragm wakeup drill - P. 148**

Exercise Description: Let's improve your body's ability to move better through breathing efficiency. Lie on your back, relax, and diaphragmatically breathe. Begin rubbing into your sternum with one or two hands (using the tips of your fingers). Next, find the base of your rib cage. Begin digging laterally under the bottom of the ribs. Pay attention to tenderness and tightness of the diaphragm. Relax and breathe through wakeup drills.

- **Upper body segmental rolling: 3 x 1 full roll each side**
  P. 149-150-151

Exercise Description: Begin by lying on your back. Lift one arm and bring it across your body. Lift your head and look in the direction you are rolling. Using your midsection muscles, slowly roll to your stomach while leading with the arm. Once on your stomach, lift one arm, look in the direction you are rolling, and bring the arm behind and across your body. Using your midsection muscles, slowly roll to your back. Be sure to keep all muscles below the waist relaxed.

- **Head nod 1 x 5 (up and down) -** P. 152-153

Exercise Description: You can execute head nods in any body position. Lie on your stomach, gaze forward. Look to the ceiling and let the head follow the eyes upward. Once at the top of a comfortable range of motion, look down toward the ground and let the head follow the eyes.

- **Half-kneeling rocking -** P. 154

Exercise Description: Begin in a half-kneeling position. Swing the top leg 90°. Lean over the top leg, feeling a stretch of the adductors of the hip. You can also keep the foot in front, lean forward, and feel the hip muscles stretch.

- **Active straight leg raise corrective 3 x 10 -** P. 143-144

- **Glute bridge 3 x 10 -** P. 145

- **Plank or modified plank 3 x :10 -** P. 155

Exercise Description: Lie on your stomach with your elbows under your shoulders and toes tucked. Bring your hips and knees off the ground so your body is in a neutral-spine position. Maintain this position for the recommended duration. Enhance core stability with increased time under tension.

- **Passive leg lowering 3 x 8 -** P. 156-157

Exercise Description: Find the corner of a wall. Lie on your back with one leg on the wall, both legs fully extended, and toes tucked toward the knees. Slowly begin lifting the down leg to an upright position and return to the starting position.

- **Cross crawl 1 x :60 -** P. 157-158

Exercise Description: Stand tall with arms extended to the ceiling. Lift one knee while bringing the opposite arm to that knee and return to the starting position. Alternate sides in a contralateral fashion.

Day 3, Day 6, and Day 7 Cardiovascular Training

Milestone #2:
Build a Stronger Core.
ZONE: CORE

1- Week strategic movement program:
   Recommended equipment: Any resist-a-band or super band

VIDEO RESOURCES:

Milestone #2 Day 1 and Day 4:
https://vimeo.com/471331552/93403537a8

Milestone #2 Day 2 and Day 5:
https://vimeo.com/471336009/2560bb4e77

Milestone #2 Day 3, Day 6, and Day 7:
https://vimeo.com/471338113/86ddc57b20

Day 1 and Day 4 Strategic Movement Session for Milestone #2:

- **Breath 1 x :60 -** P. 135

Relaxed position

- **Diaphragm wakeup drill -** P. 148

- **Psoas wakeup drill -** P. 159

Exercise Description: Lie on your back and find your belly button. Measure one inch over and one inch down and begin pushing the fingers of one hand in at a 45° angle. Place the opposite hand on top of that hand to add pressure and move the fingers in a small circle.

- **Lower body segmental rolling 3 x 1 full roll each side -** P. 136-137-138

- **Upper body segmental rolling: 3 x 1 full roll each side -** P. 149-150-151

- **Hard rolling: 1 x 1 full roll each side -** P. 160-161

Exercise Description: Lie on your back with your arms and legs fully extended. Lift your arms, legs, head, and shoulders off the ground. Look in the direction you want to roll and using your midsection muscles, roll to your side and eventually to your stomach. On your stomach, lift your extended arms and legs, look in the direction you want to roll, and using your midsection muscles, roll to your side and eventually to your back.

- **Head nod 1 x 5 (side to side) -** P. 138

- **Head nod 1 x 5 (up and down) -** P. 152-153

- **Hip rock 1 x 5 -** P. 139-140

- **Single leg hip rock 1 x 5 each -** P. 140

- **Side to side pigeon pose 1 x 5 -** P. 141-142

- **Plank or modified plank 1 x :20 -** P. 155

- **Bird dog 3 x 10 -** P. 170-171

- **Dead bug 3 x 10 -** P. 162-163

Exercise Description: Lie on your back with your arms extended toward the ceiling and legs off the ground in a 90° hip and knee position. Bring one hand to the opposite knee while extending the opposite arm and leg. Return arms and legs to the starting position and repeat or alternate in a contralateral pattern.

- **Glute bridge 3 x 10 -** P. 145

- **Hurdle step corrective 3 x 10 -** P. 164-165

Exercise Description: Attach a Cook Band or resistance band to a stable pivot point. Stand tall while grasping the band. Bring your arms to your hips, hold, breathe, and lift one knee. Return the foot to the ground and repeat or alternate legs while maintaining arm position and core activation.

- **Crawl 3 x :30 (choose the crawl appropriate for you)**

    Baby crawls: - P. 166

    Exercise Description: Begin in a tabletop position. Move your hand and opposite leg in a contralateral pattern as you baby-crawl forward, backward, or from side to side.

    Bird dog crawls: - P. 170-171

    Exercise Description: Begin in a tabletop position. Extend your arm and opposite leg fully in a contralateral pattern as you bird dog–crawl forward, backward, or from side to side.

    Leopard crawls: - P. 167-168

    Exercise Description: Begin in a tabletop position with your toes tucked. Lift your knees barely off the ground. Move your hand and opposite leg in a contralateral pattern as you leopard-crawl forward, backward, or from side to side. Keep your spine in neutral and your hips stable, and envision crawling like a prowling cat.

Spider crawls: - P. 169

Exercise Description: Similar to a leopard crawl, begin in a tabletop position with your toes tucked. Lift your knees barely off the ground and flare them to the side as you crawl. Move your hand and opposite leg in a contralateral pattern as you spider-crawl forward, backward, or from side to side. Keep your spine in neutral and your hips stable, and envision scaling a rock cliff.

Day 2 and Day 5 Strategic Movement Session for Milestone #2:

- **Breath: 1 x :60 -** P. 135

- **Diaphragm wakeup drill -** P. 148

- **RPR: Psoas wakeup drill -** P. 159

- **RPR: Glute wakeup drill -** P. 172

Exercise Description: Enhancing the reflexive neural connection to your glutes provides many benefits, such as better movement, enhanced metabolism, and reduced risk of injury. Bring your thumbs to the posterior aspect of the base of your skull. Scrape the soft tissue laterally, paying attention to any tenderness or tension.

- **Upper body segmental rolling: 3 x 1 full roll each side -** P. 149-150-151

- **Hard rolling: 1 x 1 full roll each side -** P. 160-161

- **Head nod 1 x 5 (side to side) -** P. 138

- **Head nod 1 x 5 (up and down)** - P. 152-153

- **Hip rock 1 x 5** - P. 139-140

- **Single leg hip rock 1 x 5 each** - P. 140

- **Side-to-side pigeon pose 1 x 5** - P. 141-142

- **Plank or modified plank** - P. 155

- **Bird dog 3 x 10** - P. 170-171

- **Half-kneeling pallof press** - P. 173

Exercise Description: Pallof press in any stance. Position a resistance band at chest height while in half-kneeling position. Grab the band with one hand and the opposite hand on top at the chest level. Place appropriate tension on the band and extend your arms. Pause and bring your hands back to the starting position.

- **Standing hip hinge** - P. 174-175-176

Exercise Description: Stand tall with a shoulder-width stance. Place a dowel on three attachment points: your lower back, your upper back, and your head. Position one hand in the lordosis of your cervical spine and the other in the lordosis of your lumbar spine and slowly begin bringing your hips back (hip hinging). At the same time, move your upper torso in direct opposition toward the floor. Maintain a neutral spine and comfortably bent knees. Hinge at the hips through a full range of motion, then return to the starting position.

You can load this movement when appropriate by using a band. Attach a band to a low attachment point and straddle the band.

- **Multidirectional marching** - P. 147

- **Crawl 3 x :30** - P. 166-171

(choose the crawl appropriate for you)

- Baby crawls
- Bird dog crawls
- Leopard crawls
- Spider crawls

Day 3, Day 6, and Day 7 Cardiovascular Training

Milestone #3:
Move Better by Hip Hinging.
ZONE: CORE

One-week strategic movement program:
Recommended equipment includes a resist-a-band, stability ball, and 1/2 foam roller.

VIDEO RESOURCES:

Milestone #3 Day 1 and Day 4:
https://vimeo.com/471345043/bb958d63cb

Milestone #3 Day 2 and Day 5:
https://vimeo.com/471348813/0eb613e1e4

Milestone #3 Day 3, Day 6, and Day 7:
https://vimeo.com/471351789/1d9143cbb0

Day 1 & Day 4 Strategic Movement Session For Milestone #3:

- **Breath: 1 x :60 -** P. 135
- **Diaphragm wakeup drill -** P. 148

- Psoas wakeup drill - P. 159

- Glute wakeup drill - P. 172

- Lower body segmental rolling: 1 x 1 full roll each side - P. 136-137-138

- Upper body segmental rolling: 1 x 1 full roll each side - P. 149-150-151

- Hard rolling: 1 x 1 full roll each side - P. 160-161

- Head nod 1 x 5 (side to side) - P. 138

- Head nod 1 x 5 (up and down) - P. 152-153

- Hip rock 1 x 5 - P. 139-140

- Single leg hip rock 1 x 5 each - P. 140

- Passive leg lowering 3 x 8 - P. 156-157

- Toe touch progression on 1/2 foam roller 1 x 5 - P. 177 Exercise

Description: Place your toes on the top of a 1/2 foam roller. Extend your arms to the ceiling, relax, breathe, and begin hip hinging by bringing your hips back and your arms toward your toes. Continue transitioning your hands to your toes by shifting your hips back, emphasizing an anterior pelvic tilt, chin tuck, and spine flexion. Bend your knees as much as you need to touch your toes and return to the starting position successfully.

- **Dynamic movement flows - P. 178-183**

Exercise Description: Movement flows are vast. Here are a few examples of movement flows we use to increase body temperature, enhance mobility, and prepare for training.

Cross leg tap: Stand tall and lift one leg fully extended while touching with the opposite hand.

Ankle grab: Stand tall, grab one ankle, pull into the glute, push the hips forward, and reach toward the ceiling with the opposite arm.

Single leg hip hinge: Keep one foot on the ground while you aggressively hip-hinge. Get your torso as close to parallel to the floor as you can comfortably.

Ankle grab with hip hinge

Dynamic glute stretch: Stand tall and cross one leg over the other knee. Sit and feel a glute stretch. You can also grab the foot and knee simultaneously to feel a glute stretch.

Hamstring: Stand tall and extend one leg with heel down and toe up. Hip-hinge aggressively and maintain a neutral spine.

- **Crawl 3 x :30 (choose the crawl appropriate for you) -** P. 166-171
    - Baby crawls
    - Leopard crawls
    - Bird dog crawls
    - Spider crawls

Day 2 and Day 5 Strategic Movement Session for Milestone #3:

- **Breath: 1 x :60 -** P. 135
- **Diaphragm wakeup drill -** P. 148
- **Psoas wakeup drill -** P. 159
- **Glute wakeup drill -** P. 172

- **Lateral Sling Wakeup Drill -** P. 184

Exercise Description: Lie on your back. Find the top of your hip with each thumb. Begin scraping the edge of the entire hip. Wakeup drills feel uncomfortable, so try to relax and breathe as you dig in.

- **Lower-body segmental rolling: 1 x 1 full roll each side -** P. 136-137-138

- **Upper-body segmental rolling: 1 x 1 full roll each side -** P. 149-150-151

- **Hard rolling: 1 x 1 full roll each side -** P. 160-161

- **Hip rock 1 x 5 -** P. 139-140

- **Single leg hip rock 1 x 5 each -** P. 140

- **Resisted push toe touch 2 x 5 -** P. 185

Exercise Description: Set a resistance band at the knee to hip height. Perform a toe touch and push against the band as you touch your toes. This movement activates your core and should help you pattern the toe touch.

- **Resist-a-ball isometric core stability 2 x 5 -** P. 186

Exercise Description: Lie on your back with your arms extended toward the ceiling and your hips and knees bent at 90°. You can use a stability ball to bring all extremities in toward each other. This exercise is an isometric exercise with many options. You can activate spiral lines with opposite arms and legs, obliques with the same side arm and leg, and the entire core with all extremities.

- **Single leg Romanian deadlift 2 x 5 -** P. 187-188

Exercise Description: Stand tall. Begin by bringing one leg behind you as you hip-hinge aggressively. Slowly hinge and get your torso as close to parallel to the ground as possible.

- **Dynamic movement flows - P. 178-183**
  - Cross-leg tap
  - Ankle grab with hip hinge
  - Dynamic glute stretch
  - Dynamic hamstring stretch
- **Crawl 3 x :30 (choose the crawl appropriate for you) - P. 166-171**
  - Baby crawls
  - Leopard crawls
  - Bird dog crawls
  - Spider crawls

Day 3, Day 6, & Day 7 Cardiovascular Training

Milestone #4:
Improve Your Posture.

ZONE: SPINE

One-week strategic movement program:
Recommended equipment includes a foam roller and dowel.

VIDEO RESOURCES:

Milestone #4 Day 1, Day 3, and Day 5:
https://vimeo.com/471359924/d6eaca8406
Milestone #4 Day 2, Day 4, Day 6, and Day 7: Cardiovascular exercise

Day 1, Day 3, and Day 5 Strategic Movement Session for Milestone #4:

GOLDEN RULE #1: Stand tall.

GOLDEN RULE #2: Build midsection stability in neutral spine.

- **Perpendicular passive posture corrective w/breath 1x2:00+ - P. 189**

Exercise Description: Lie on your back with a dowel or small cylindrical object perpendicular to your thoracic spine. Be sure the object is not too large. Relax and breathe and let your spine extend around the object. Periodically move the dowel higher on the spine one vertebrae at a time.

- **Parallel passive posture corrective on foam roller w/ breath - P. 190**

Exercise Description: Lie on a foam roller with your elbows at a 90° angle. Relax and breathe.

- **Myofascial preparation—entire backside chain - P. 191-192-193**

Exercise Description: Muscles tend to tighten and develop neural abnormalities through training, stress, excessive sitting, or poor biomechanics. Myofascial release places pressure on muscles, creating a reflexive response that aids in proper muscle function. Use a foam roll, stick, or massage to put pressure on muscles of the backside chain. These muscles tend to tighten through daily living. Breathe and relax as you "roll" and place pressure on tight muscles and tender points.

- **Foam roll thoracic extension - P. 194**

Exercise Description: Lie perpendicular with your thoracic spine on a foam roller. Hold your head in your hands and bring your elbows closer. Gently lift your elbows, extending your spine, then return to the starting position.

- **Bird dog 3 x 5 - P. 170-171**

- **Wall angel (floor or wall) 3 x 5 - P. 219**

Exercise Description: You can perform this exercise on a wall or the floor. Position your arms in a goalpost position with your elbows at 90°.

Keep your elbows and wrists on the wall (or floor) and begin moving your arms upward. Go through a full range of motion, then return to the starting position.

- **Skydiver 3 x :20 -** P. 195

Exercise Description: Lie on your stomach with your arms and legs at 45° angles, much like a star. Lift your arms, legs, and head off the ground, so that your backside muscles are activated. Hold this position and breathe. Avoid excessive extension of the spine.

- **Crawl 3 x :30 (choose the crawl appropriate for you) -** P. 166-171
  - Baby crawls
  - Leopard crawls
  - Bird dog crawls
  - Spider crawls

Day 2, Day 4, Day 6, and Day 7 Cardiovascular Training

Milestone #5:
Find Shoulder Mobility.

ZONE: SPINE

One-week strategic movement program:
Recommended equipment includes a foam roll and Indian clubs.

VIDEO RESOURCES:

Milestone #5 Day 1, Day 3, and Day 5:
https://vimeo.com/471370050/da1833dd92

Milestone #5 Day 2, Day 4, Day 6, and Day 7: Cardiovascular exercise

Day 1, Day 3, and Day 5 Strategic Movement Session for Milestone #5:

GOLDEN RULE #1: Avoid loaded overhead pressing.
GOLDEN RULE #2: Master Milestone #4.

- **Breath: 1 x :60 -** P. 135

- **Diaphragm wakeup drill -** P. 148

- **Shoulder wakeup drill -** P. 196

Exercise Description: Lie on your back and reach one hand across your body on your ribs. Position your hand as if it were a tiger claw and scrape or pull the hand across your rib cage. Repeat.

- **Supraspinatus wakeup drill -** P. 197

Exercise Description: Position your hand as a saw and place on the front of your shoulder where your arm meets your torso. Begin "sawing" the soft tissue.

- **Neck wakeup drill -** P. 197-198

Exercise Description: Find your clavicle bones with the tips of your fingers. Begin scraping just beneath the clavicles with one or both hands.

- **Myofascial prep—around shoulder (traps/lats/chest) -** P. 198

Exercise Description: Use myofascial tools such as softballs, sticks, Backnobber, or massage therapy to incorporate the myofascial release of the muscles surrounding the shoulder joint.

- **Stretch chest (doorway) -** P. 199

Exercise Description: Find a wall or doorway and place your hands above your shoulders in the doorway or on the wall. Lean forward and stretch the chest and shoulders.

- **Arm sweeps 3 x 8 -** P. 200-201-202

Exercise Description: Lie on your back with one leg across your body on a platform or stability ball. Extend your opposite arm fully with your upper back on the ground. Begin "sweeping" the arm from the top of your head to your lower back. Try to keep your shoulders, elbow, and wrist on the ground during this sweeping motion. When your arm transitions toward your back, keep your palm down. When your arm is transitioning toward your head, keep your palm up.

- **Indian clubs -** P. 203

Exercise Description: Use Indian clubs to enhance the mobility of your shoulder joints. Indian clubs provide traction of the shoulder joints during circular motions. Play with this and have fun!

- **Crawl 3 x :30 (choose the crawl appropriate for you) -** P. 166-171
  - Baby crawls
  - Leopard crawls
  - Bird dog crawls
  - Spider crawls

Day 2, Day 4, Day 6, and Day 7 Cardiovascular Training

Milestone #6:
Establish Thoracic Rotation.

ZONE: SPINE

One-week strategic movement program:

VIDEO RESOURCES:

Milestone #6 Day 1, Day 3, and Day 5:
https://vimeo.com/471375227/f638fb797d

Milestone #6 Day 2, Day 4, Day 6, and Day 7: Cardiovascular exercise

Day 1, Day 3, & Day 5 Strategic Movement Session For Milestone #6

- **Breath: 1 x :60 -** P. 135
- **Diaphragm wakeup drill -** P. 148
- **Shoulder wakeup drill -** P. 196
- **Supraspinatus wakeup drill -** P. 197
- **Neck wakeup drill -** P. 197-198
- **RPR: Lats wakeup drill -** P. 204

Exercise Description: Locate the base of your rib cage. Move up three ribs and locate a slight indention of the rib cage. Drill in with your thumb while you breathe and relax.

- **Foam-roll thoracic spine -** P. 205

Exercise Description: Place your thoracic spine perpendicular to a foam roll with your hands supporting your head. Roll back and forth through the mid-spine.

- **Quadruped t-spine rotation with hand on neck or hand on lower back, palm up -** P. 206-207

Exercise Description: This exercise can be done with the hand behind the head or arm extended. Start in a tabletop position. Sit on your heels and place one hand behind your head. Begin rotating toward the ceiling with your eyes and elbow. When you reach a full range of motion, begin turning toward the opposite hand and repeat.

- **Brettzel -** P. 208

Exercise Description: Lie on your side and grab your lower leg/ankle with your topside hand. Bring your back and shoulders to the ground as you bend your topside leg. Position your bottom-side hand on your topside knee. Breathe and relax as you hold this stretch.

- **Crawl 3 x :30 (choose the crawl appropriate for you)** - P. 166-171
  - Baby crawls
  - Bird dog crawls
  - Leopard crawls
  - Spider crawls

Day 2, Day 4, Day 6, and Day 7 Cardiovascular Training

Milestone #7:
Improve Mobility from the Ground Up.

ZONE: MOVEMENT

One-week strategic movement program:
Recommended equipment includes a foam roller.

VIDEO RESOURCES:

Milestone #7 Day 1, Day 3, and Day 5:
https://vimeo.com/471379498/6ba456d3f7

Milestone #7 Day 2, Day 4, Day 6, and Day 7: Cardiovascular exercise

Day 1, Day 3, and Day 5 Strategic Movement Session for Milestone #7:

- **Breath: 1 x :60** - P. 135
- **Diaphragm wakeup drill** - P. 148
- **Shoulder wakeup drill** - P. 196

- **Gastrocnemius wakeup drill - P. 209**

Exercise Description: Lie on your side. Using your thumb, find a point just below your rib cage toward your belly button on your front side. On the other hand, using the thumb, find a position on the back that is directly in opposition to your front-side point. Drill your thumbs toward each other.

- **Myofascial prep - plantar fascia - P. 210**

Exercise Description: Use a golf ball or object that provides appropriate pressure for your plantar fascia. Place your foot on the object and massage the entire plantar fascia.

- **Passive foot range of motion - P. 211**

Exercise Description: Use your hands to stretch the joints of the foot in flexion and extension. These joints include the ankle, interphalangeal joints, metatarsophalangeal joints, and tarsometatarsal joints.

- **Active foot range of motion - P. 212**

Exercise Description: Move your foot and ankle through a full flexion and extension range of motion.

- **Gastrocnemius/ankle Stretch - P. 213**

Exercise Description: Sit on a stability ball. Bring one heel into the stability ball as far as possible. Begin shifting your body weight over the heel to stretch the soft tissue of the lower posterior leg.

- **Hip rocking with ankle sit and focused breath - P. 139-140**

- **Crawl 3 x :30 (choose the crawl appropriate for you) - P. 166-171**
    - Baby crawls
    - Leopard crawls
    - Bird dog crawls
    - Spider crawls

Day 2, Day 4, Day 6, and Day 7 Cardiovascular Training

Milestone #8:
Pattern the Squat.

ZONE: MOVEMENT

One-week strategic movement program:
Recommended equipment includes a Cook Band.

VIDEO RESOURCES:
Milestone #8 Day 1, Day 3, and Day 5:
https://vimeo.com/471389126/cecafa7f1d

Milestone #8 Day 2, Day 4, Day 6, and Day 7: Cardiovascular exercise

Day 1, Day 3, and Day 5 Corrective Training Session for Milestone #8:

- **Breath: 1 x :60 -** P. 135
- **Diaphragm wakeup drill -** P. 148
- **Psoas wakeup drill -** P. 159
- **Glute wakeup drill -** P. 172
- **Quadriceps wakeup drill -** P. 218

Exercise Description: Lie on your back. Find the space between the top of your hip and the bottom of your rib cage. Using your thumb as a hook, begin pulling the tissue across the body repeatedly. Wakeup drills feel uncomfortable, so try to relax and breathe as you dig in.

- **Lateral sling wakeup drill -** P. 184
- **Gastrocnemius wakeup drill -** P. 209

- **Lats wakeup drill -** P. 204

- **Abdominal wakeup drill -** P. 214

Exercise Description: Chop the inside of your legs from your knees to your groin.

- **Shoulder wakeup drill -** P. 196

- **Supraspinatus wakeup drill -** P. 197

- **Neck wakeup drill -** P. 197-198

- **Rolling patterns 3 x 1 you choose the type:**

- **Lower body segmental rolling: 1 x 1 full roll each side -** P. 136-137-

- **Upper body segmental rolling: 1 x 1 full roll each side -** P. 149-150-151

- **Hard rolling: 1 x 1 full roll each side -** P. 160-161

- **Assisted deep squat patterning 3 x 5 -** P. 215

Exercise Description: Find a pole. Begin in a squat stance with your hands on the pole. Slide your hands down the pole as you squat toward your ankles. Maintain a neutral spine, keep your heels on the ground, relax, and breathe. Pause at the bottom and return to the starting position.

- **Squat patterning with bodyweight 3 x 10 (paying attention to each aspect of the squat) -** P. 216-217

Exercise Description: Start in a squat stance (feet slightly wider than shoulder-width with your toes pointed out comfortably) with your arms extended for a counterbalance. Initiate the movement with your hips and begin squatting. Try to keep your torso upright and spine in neutral as you squat. Your thighs are parallel to the ground at the bottom of the squat. Return to the starting position by driving your hips, standing tall, and swimming the arms to your hips. Get your breath in sequence with the movement pattern by exhaling on exertion. You should feel your glutes and core activation at the top of the squat pattern.

- **Crawl 3 x :30 (choose the crawl appropriate for you) -** P. 166-171
    - Baby crawls
    - Leopard crawls
    - Bird dog crawls
    - Spider crawls

Day 2, Day 4, Day 6, and Day 7 Cardiovascular Training

Milestone #9:
Apply the Squat and Connect to Strength.
ZONE: MOVEMENT

Strategic Movement Program: Begin following the secret sauce with modifications for kettlebell skills.

*As you transition to Milestones #10 through #21, you'll follow the secret sauce programming. In the program, you'll notice many kettlebell skills, such as swings, cleans, snatches, and Turkish get-ups. These movements require professional guidance for safety and efficiency. We follow StrongFirst standards and recommend trained and experienced coaches who are form fanatics.

SPORT SPECIFICITY

Reaching Milestone #21 is only the beginning for those looking to improve sport-specific performance. Transforming the body through milestones creates injury resiliency and optimizes human performance. Begin transitioning your movement, strength, and power into basketball, tennis, golf, mixed martial arts, football, cycling, baseball, running, or any other activity you enjoy or in which you compete.

TRAINING SESSION DETAILS

We reach peak physiological functioning in our mid-twenties according to Human Development: A Life-Span View by Robert Kail and John Cavanaugh. You might jump right into your workout if you were anything like me when I was at Washington State University or Indiana University. Our standard warmup back then included getting together with five others and sprinting across a basketball court in Wildermuth Gym at Indiana University. Today, at fifty years of age, it wouldn't be smart for me to do that. Instead, I have to train smarter because my body requires it. I can still perform at a high level, but the way I get there is different from when I was in my twenties. Train smart to reduce the risk of injury and perform at your best.

For our program, a typical small group session runs about forty-five minutes. Each session is unique; however, we can begin to construct a general outline of our sessions.

Here's a snapshot of what that might look like:

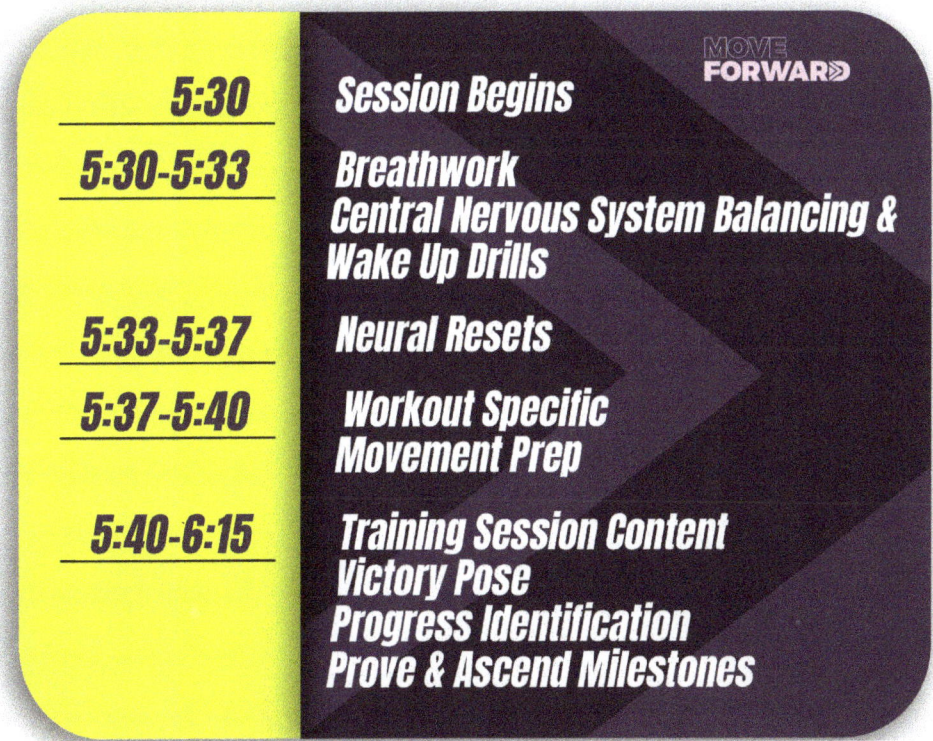

SECRET SAUCE PROGRAMMING

Optimizing behaviors is the name of the game if you want to make progress with weight loss, fat loss, and body composition change. These behaviors include getting restorative sleep, managing life stress, eating clean foods, practicing strategic movement, and performing cardiovascular exercise. We specialize in identifying progress through personalized strategic movement sessions. When you participate in strategic movement sessions, you'll begin integrating our "Secret Sauce."

The secret sauce is the programming our coaches follow within each session. This programming represents a basic framework. Personalize based on the milestone and your fitness level. Let's take a deeper dive into the ingredients found within the secret sauce.

1. The secret sauce includes the evolution of exercise science over the last thirty years.

We aren't guessing when we follow proven systems. The combination and influence of spine research from Dr. Stuart McGill (Back Fit Pro), human functional movement from Gray Cook (Functional Movement Systems), neural resets from Tim Anderson (Original Strength), central nervous system correctives from Chris Scott (Neurosomatic Balancing), reflexive wakeup drills from Chris Korfist (Reflexive Performance Resets), and strength and power principles and kettlebell skills from Pavel Tsatsouline (Strongfirst) make the secret sauce much more than a workout of the day. A workout just to entertain you or make you "feel the burn" isn't an effective strategy for progress.

2. The secret sauce optimizes recovery.

Yes, recovery is critical to a consistent exercise routine. Without healing, your body plateaus, and the risk of injury skyrockets. We recommend incorporating a strategic movement stimulus every other day (three days per week). Simultaneously, alternate cardiovascular exercise and increase to a near-daily schedule (based upon the outcome you are looking for).

3. The secret sauce is body-friendly.

Most barbell movements, burpees, extreme spinal extension, sit-ups, upright rows, isolated joint movements, ballistic side bends and excessive spine rotation, timing workouts, and crunches are all things you won't see within the secret sauce.

What will you experience?

A. A smart start that neurally connects the body through breath, central nervous system optimization, wakeup drills, and neural resets.

B. An emphasis on neutral spine and core stability throughout the session.

C. Inspiration to challenge yourself and make it doable.

D. Encouragement to load proficient movement patterns when appropriate.

E. Skill breakdown drills to improve form and enhance effectiveness.

4. The secret sauce promotes energy system utilization to enhance physiological adaptation.

Our bodies use alactic, anaerobic, and aerobic energy systems to handle the challenges presented within each session. The sessions complement one another as you go from session to session, week to week, and month to month. When you follow the three-days-per-week program, all three energy systems work in a way that promotes physiological adaptation, such as better movement, more stamina, greater strength, and enhanced shape and tone.

5. The program variables change from week to week while maintaining the foundational movements and schemes.

This step-by-step progress as you go from session to session brings about predictable physiological adaptations. When you see increases in your repetitions, for example, from eight to ten to twelve to fifteen, it promotes muscle endurance. When you see decreases in repetitions such as ten to eight to six to four, it promotes strength. When you see conditioning schemes such as: :30, :40, :60 seconds or longer worth of sprints, battle ropes, swings, vertical jumps, or jumping jacks, this promotes stamina. The opposite approach to this programming is to offer a random workout of the day. Although there is intrigue and surprise with a workout of the day, there is no predictability in the results.

6. Periodization is the backbone.

The secret sauce program is a macrocycle that is six months long. Each macrocycle has six mesocycles lasting four weeks each. Each mesocycle has four micro-cycles (weeks), with three strategic movement sessions: These training sessions progress weekly, optimizing energy systems and recovery.

Here's a visual to help you understand the secret sauce programming. In the strength coaching world, it is called periodization.

6 MONTHS
MACROCYCLE

MESOCYCLE

| JAN | FEB | MAR | APR | MAY | JUN |

MICROCYCLES

WEEK 1 | WEEK 2 | WEEK 3 | WEEK 4 | WEEK 1 | WEEK 2 | WEEK 3 | WEEK 4 | WEEK 1 | WEEK 2 | WEEK 3 | WEEK 4 | WEEK 1 | WEEK 2 | WEEK 3 | WEEK 4 | WEEK 1 | WEEK 2 | WEEK 3 | WEEK 4 | WEEK 1 | WEEK 2 | WEEK 3 | WEEK 4

INDIVIDUAL SESSIONS

CARDIOVASCULAR EXERCISE IS THE MIRACLE CURE

The last, but certainly not the least of the behaviors to optimize is cardiovascular exercise. There are vast amounts of research that document the need for each of us to consistently provide adequate cardiorespiratory movement to improve our health and move toward our goals.

Like every behavior, you must personalize the recommendation based on your health history, current fitness level, and goals. Commit to moving your body daily. Work with your primary coach to determine your cardiovascular program's exact duration, mode, frequency, and intensity. Please note: Your cardiovascular program variables change over time as your fitness level improves.

Since you'll be integrating three days per week of strategic movement into your schedule, our baseline and general recommendation for cardiovascular exercise is as follows:

Frequency: Four days per week.

Mode: Anything you find practical and doable, including walking, running, cycling, swimming, elliptical, stair-stepping, rowing, or any other form of continuous, large-muscle, rhythmic movement.

Duration: Begin with twenty minutes, including a warmup and a cooldown, and gradually increase the time to forty-three minutes or more.

Intensity: Use a rating of perceived exertion scale from 1 to 10. This scale is known as the Borg Scale, developed by Swedish researcher Gunnar Borg. Perform steady-state cardiovascular exercise at an intensity of 4 to 7. In essence, exercise until you can still talk, but you'd rather not.

RATING OF PERCEIVED EXERTION SCALE		HR & POWER ZONES	TRAINING EXAMPLES
RPE 1	Very Easy	Active Recovery	All day pace. 30-90 min easy rides
RPE 2	Easy	Endurance	Long slow distance, walking, light flexibility work
RPE 3	Moderate		Long steady aerobic endurance training, light yoga
RPE 4		Tempo	Hiking moderate terrain, tepo riding 60-80 min
RPE 5	Hard		Strength endurance training
RPE 6	Very Hard	Threshold	10-30 min running or cycling intervals
RPE 7		Vo2 Max	3-8 min work intervals
RPE 8	Extremely Difficult	Anaerobic Capacity	Strength & power training, mountain running. 30 sec to 3 min max efforts
RPE 9			
RPE 10	Max Effort	Neuromuscular Power	Max lifts, sprinting 10 seconds or under

COLLABORATION AND ACCOUNTABILITY THROUGH CONNECT SESSIONS

"Accountability is the key to personal success." —Susan Scott, in her book Fierce Conversations

Connect sessions are the glue that holds everything together. There's a reason elite athletes and business leaders have mentors and coaches. We believe that if you could do it on your own, you would have done it already.

Connect sessions create a collaborative relationship that identifies progress and propels personal growth. Meeting with your primary coach weekly is ideal for monitoring progress, discussing experiences, and establishing strategies. Move Forward is a process that requires guidance, support, and motivation to confront villains, understand setbacks, develop strategies, achieve milestones, and overcome challenges.

According to the Psychology Dictionary Professional Reference, two motivation systems govern human behavior: the behavioral inhibition system and the behavioral activation system. The behavioral inhibition system exhibits negative emotionality, with restraint in responding to the world. The behavioral approach system activates by incentive motivation. The response is toward the stimuli as something desired. Move Forward and personal wellness coaching taps into the behavioral approach system, delivering power over powerlessness to move you toward your potential.

"A goal without a plan is just a wish." —Antoine de Saint-Exupery

Your primary coach sets up your online personal wellness platform and uses the science of behavior-change to motivate, enhance awareness, bring mindfulness, and deliver winning strategies on your journey to extraordinary living.

To do this, your primary coach uses the Move Forward navigation mechanism, which includes key elements revolving around the specific actions of the milestones. The milestones and behaviors enable health and wellness, in conjunction with deep human connections, to drive happiness. Passion drives fulfillment and unearthing your purpose brings rise to extraordinary living. These elements coordinate and give rise to an extraordinary life. Let's analyze the elements and present the infographic.

PURPOSE: Reason/Desire/Aspiration/Intent

PASSION: Spirit/Zeal/Dedication/Joy/Dharma

FULFILLMENT: Gratification/Achievement/Contentment

HAPPINESS: Joy/Pleasure/Enjoyment/Optimism

HEALTH: Energy/Strength/Fitness/Vigor

WELLNESS: Vitality/Well-Being/Wholeness

DEEP HUMAN CONNECTION: Engagement/Love/Care/Understanding/Empathy/Community

PRESENTING THE NAVIGATION MECHANISM TO EXTRAORDINARY LIVING FOUND AT THE CENTER OF MOVE FORWARD

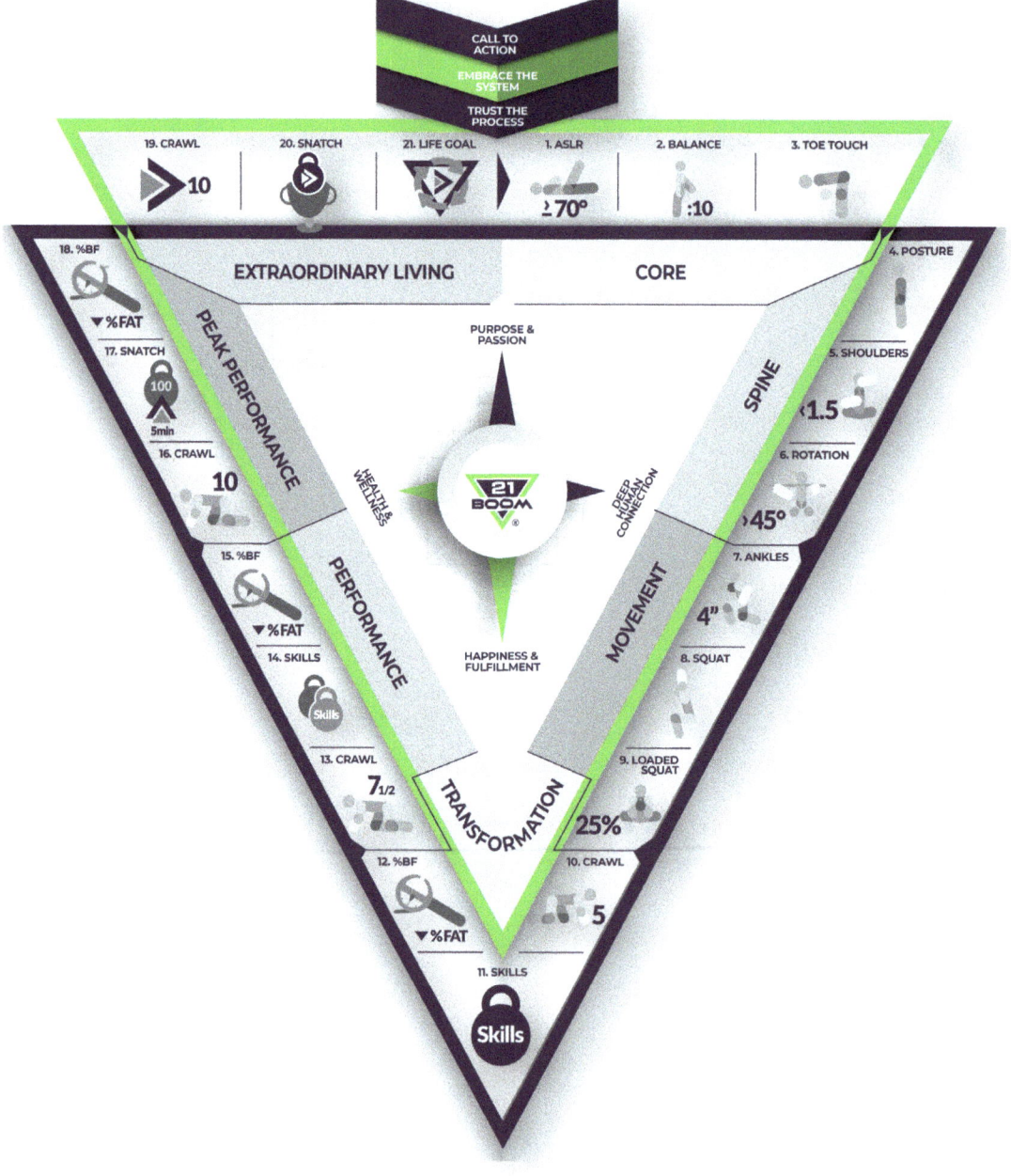

There you have it: the navigation mechanism and path to extraordinary living. This is by far the greatest gift I could give to the industry to which I have devoted an entire lifetime. It wasn't the money or external reward, it was a silent and relentless calling that I now realize was bigger than myself, and it had to find the light of day. It represents the crowning achievement of my life's work, and I'm hopeful that it inspires you to make an impact upon your society. To be able to share how this system ultimately led me to live my life in the most fulfilling way possible—that is the driving force behind this book. I feel this is a reciprocal relationship; I am giving what I have learned to others, and I look forward to their successes, which will eventually lead to them giving back the best of themselves to this world we all share.

We've provided a Milestone Details chart on **P. 220-222** for a quick summary and review when needed.

CHERISH EACH DAY: START AND FINISH STRONG

Prioritizing your health and investing your time to Move Forward will make the difference between where you are today and living that extraordinary life. Let's construct the bookends of your day, and then we'll unveil a 7-Day Behavioral Blueprint.

In his book *Entrepreneur Vitality*, Jake Havron describes the concept of bookends when planning your day. These bookends enable you to biohack your body through morning and evening habits that become rituals.

Here's a 4-Step Waking Ritual We Recommend:

A. Rise, stand tall, and enhance your state of mind.

B. Begin a breathing practice.

There are many resources available to understand the importance of breathing and meditation. For starters, stand, sit, or lie on your back and follow these steps.

- Relax. Let your body melt into the floor.
- Get in touch with any deep and chronic tension through the glutes and upper back, then let go and relax.
- Begin bringing your awareness to your breath.
- Inhale and exhale through the nose.
- Bring your breath to the pelvic floor.
- Feel your belly rising and falling with each inhalation and exhalation.
- Slow your breathing and calm your body. Your inhale may last for roughly three seconds while your exhale may last for five seconds. Dr. Alan Watkins, the founder of Complete Coherence recommends rhythmic, smooth, and heart-centered breathing to set the table for positive emotional states.
- Continue to relax, breathe, and let your mind experience the sensation of mindful breathing and the connection to the earth, or let it roam without borders.

C. Practice gratitude, ending with "I love my life."

Practicing gratitude is an extremely effective strategy, recommended by Adam Markel in his book *Pivot*.

D. Visualize your day and make declarations.

Declarations are similar to ordering food at a restaurant. Declare what you want and how you are going to get it.

Another great resource is *The Miracle Morning* by Hal Elrod. You'll learn to incorporate his SAVERS morning routine for focus and balance.

Between the bookends of your day, you'll want to be as productive as possible. Work with your body and embrace productivity strategies. Two strategies we recommend include identifying your top priority and focusing mentally using durational increments optimal for you.

In the book *The One Thing*, Gary Keller describes the importance of identifying the one thing that will move everything else forward. It is somewhat like finding the first domino in a room of dominoes: When you find the first domino, all the other dominoes will then begin to fall. When you make a list of the most important things to tackle, beginning with your top priority, you're assured a productive day.

> "Spend your time on things that matter."
> —Laura Vanderkam, time management consultant

Here's a 4-Step Evening Ritual We Recommend:

A. Review and update your personal wellness platform.

In essence, look back on your day and document what went well and according to plan.

B. Connect emotionally with those most important to you.

C. Incorporate a technology detox.

D. Begin a meditation practice.

It is normal to be skeptical of these strategies. Just like thousands of people before you, however, when you practice them, you'll begin experiencing more happiness, greater clarity, higher levels of peacefulness, better sleep, and much more.

THE 7-DAY BEHAVIORAL BLUEPRINT

Here is an example of an ideal week; it should be modified to fit your life.

Sunday—PREP FOR THE WEEK

- Review your plan on your personal wellness platform and schedule training sessions.
- Prepare your environment by shopping for clean food.
- Be mindful and present, and prepare to identify and declare progress.

Monday—DAY 1

5:30 a.m.: Waking ritual

6:00 a.m.: Strategic movement session

8:00 a.m.: Productivity hacking

- Identify your number-one priority for the day.
- Break the day into distraction-free segments.

6:00 p.m.: Your main meal with family. Eliminate calories and begin fasting after dinner. Drink water.

9:30 p.m.: Evening ritual

10:00 p.m.: Sleep

Nutrition: Listen to your body and eat whole and natural foods when your body needs them. Identify your fasting duration. From Sunday evening meal to Monday's first food, how many hours were you in a fasting state? An example may be "from 7 p.m. dinner to 7 a.m. breakfast," which would be twelve hours.

Tuesday—DAY 2

5:30 a.m.: Waking ritual

6:00 a.m.: Cardiovascular exercise

8:00 a.m.: Productivity hacking

- Identify your number-one priority for the day.
- Break the day into distraction-free segments.

6:00 p.m.: Your main meal with family. Eliminate calories and begin fasting after dinner. Drink water.

9:30 p.m.: Evening ritual

10:00 p.m.: Sleep

Nutrition: Listen to your body and eat whole and natural foods when your body needs them. Try to increase your fasting state 10 percent. If you use the above example of twelve hours, you would extend the fasting state to at least thirteen hours.

Wednesday–DAY 3

5:30 a.m.: Waking ritual

6:00 a.m.: Strategic movement session

- Identify your number-one priority for the day.
- Break the day into distraction-free segments.

6:00 p.m.: Your main meal with family. Eliminate calories and begin fasting after dinner. Drink water.

9:30 p.m: Evening ritual

10:00 p.m.: Sleep

Nutrition: Listen to your body and eat whole and natural foods when your body needs them. Try to increase your fasting state by 10 percent. If you use the example above, you would extend the fasting state to about 14.5 hours.

Thursday–DAY 4

5:30 a.m.: Waking ritual

6:00 a.m.: Cardiovascular exercise

8:00 a.m.: Productivity hacking

- Identify your number-one priority for the day.
- Break the day into distraction-free segments.

6:00 p.m: Your main meal with family. Eliminate calories and begin fasting after dinner. Drink water.

9:30 p.m.: Evening ritual

10:00 p.m.: Sleep

Nutrition: Listen to your body and eat whole and natural foods when your body needs them. Try to increase your fasting state by 10 percent. If you use the example above, you would extend the fasting state to more than fifteen hours.

Friday—DAY 5

5:30 a.m.: Waking ritual

6:00 a.m.: Strategic movement session

- Identify your number-one priority for the day.
- Break the day into distraction-free segments.

6:00 p.m.: Your main meal with family. Eliminate calories and begin fasting after dinner. Drink water.

9:30 p.m.: Evening ritual

10:00 p.m.: Sleep

Nutrition: Listen to your body and eat whole and natural foods when your body needs them. Try to increase your fasting state by 10 percent. If you use the example above, you would extend the fasting state to sixteen hours—or whatever your body is telling you. For some, an ideal fasting state might be fifteen hours, and for others, it might be twelve. Listen to your body and identify what is optimal for you based upon the outcomes you are measuring.

Saturday—DAY 6

7:00 a.m.: Waking ritual

Prioritization: Spend time on things that matter.

6:00 p.m.: Your main meal with family. Eliminate calories and begin fasting after dinner. Drink water.

9:30 p.m.: Evening ritual

10:00 p.m.: Sleep

Nutrition: Listen to your body and eat whole and natural foods when your body needs them. Perform cardiovascular exercise at a time that is convenient for you and preferably with others.

Sunday—DAY 7

7:00 a.m.: Waking ritual: Celebrate and practice gratitude for finishing your first week. This seven-day behavioral blueprint is the lifestyle required to live an extraordinary life.

Prioritization: Spend time on things that matter.

6:00 p.m: Your main meal with family. Eliminate calories and begin fasting after dinner. Drink water.

9:30 p.m.: Evening ritual

10:00 p.m.: Sleep

Nutrition: Listen to your body and eat whole and natural foods when your body needs them. Perform cardiovascular exercise at a time that is convenient for you and preferably with others.

SUMMARY

I've taken you through how Move Forward will transform your life, milestone by milestone. I've shown you how these steps will create an extraordinary life by giving you a foundation of strength in your body and mind. I've shown how this program integrates decades of research on how to reach peak physical and mental performance. You've seen how personalized coaching for your unique journey is the key to success and how it has transformed individual lives in a profound manner.

NOW, what will it look like if you decide to MOVE FORWARD?

I'm inviting you to answer the call and begin your journey to extraordinary living. Take a look at **https://www.21-boom.com** and sign up for a complimentary consultation today.

Here's what you'll get when you participate on the **21BOOM** online personal wellness platform:

- A personalized movement approach through the milestones.
- All the benefits of the secret sauce: feel good, look great, and perform your best.
- Ultimate convenience and comfort from your home.
- The 21BOOM APP to educate and track progress.
- The 21BOOM on-demand resources.
- Live coaching for guidance and motivation.
- A community of like-minded training partners.
- Connect sessions for strategy and accountability.
- Meditation and yoga sessions.

DISCLAIMER AND MEDICAL ADVICE

We recommend physician approval and a Functional Movement Screen before undertaking any exercise program. The recommendations provided are not medical guidelines and are for educational purposes only. You must consult your physician before starting any exercise program.

Complete a medical checkup with your physician before starting any exercise program. If you are taking any medications, you must consult your physician before exercising. If you experience any lightheadedness, dizziness, or shortness of breath at any time during a workout, stop the exercise immediately and see your physician.

Seek a physical examination if you are sedentary, are overweight, or have high cholesterol, high blood pressure, or diabetes.

All exercise has inherent risks. We encourage every client to take responsibility for their own safety and know their limits before performing any training program exercises. Be sure that you do not take risks that exceed your level of experience, aptitude, training, and fitness. The exercises in this program are not intended as a substitute for any exercise routine, treatment, or dietary regimen that may have been prescribed by your physician. Don't lift heavy weights if you are alone, inexperienced, injured, or tired. Don't perform any exercise without proper professional instruction. Professional instruction emphasizes form and spine-safe body mechanics. Perform wakeup drills, neural resets, and movement flows before all forms of training.

Words from Others

"Never before in the history of the world has personalized, live coaching been available so easily and so cheaply because of personal wellness platforms like 21BOOM. We are lucky to be living in the dawn of the future of fitness! Barriers to convenience are a HUGE reason people FAIL to maintain consistency with exercise, and 21BOOM dismantles that barrier!" —Anna Lotto

"The 21BOOM system is unparalleled within the fitness industry. I've been involved with many successful gym and coaching organizations over my career, and not one comes close to the comprehensive depth and systematic framework being offered to both clients and coaches. If the industry could utilize this as the gold standard, the coaching profession would prosper, and the impact upon society would be extraordinary and everlasting. This has the potential to change everything!" —Jon Hughey, thirty-year fitness center owner, manager, and coach

"Move Forward is a comprehensive and highly effective system. The framework is clear and efficient, with milestones that provide personalization and progression for each client and keep them on track and focused on the next step in the process. It easily establishes a starting point for every client, no matter what their situation is, whether that be someone old or young, sedentary or extremely active, someone new to fitness or a longtime athlete. It boils down all the important information into an actionable, step-by-step process that I have found to be very successful for my clients, helping them reach their fitness goals." —Dean Pasquerella, nuclear engineer and lifestyle coach

"The Move Forward framework is something I've been searching for throughout my entire coaching career. I wanted a fitness system that ties together safety and movement cohesively for clients to have guaranteed success. The Milestones and the interlaced proven systems are a game-changer." —Rachel Renshaw, lifestyle coach

"Game changer!" —Zack Feeney, lifestyle coach

"Work out smarter, so you can play harder." —Ryan Clark, artist and songwriter

"If I had known this stuff years ago, my joints wouldn't be in the shape they're in now." —E.C. Stumpf, powerlifter and powerlifting coach (730# deadlift personal best)

EXERCISE GALLERY

21 BOOM

BREATH

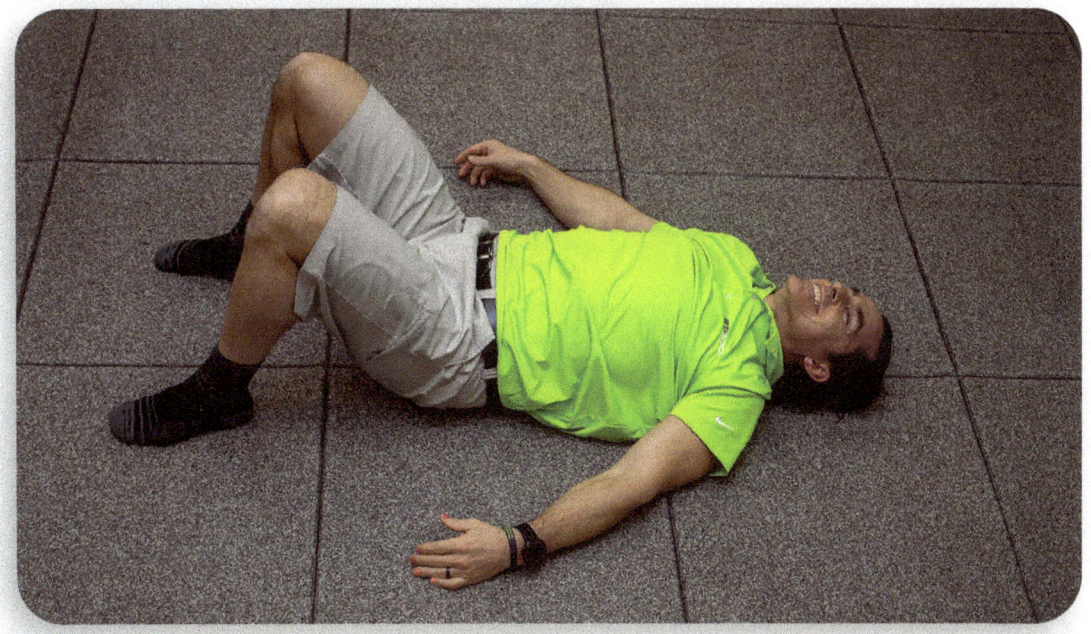

Exercise Description:

Lie on your back with your arms, legs, and head in a relaxed position.

LOWER BODY SEGMENTAL ROLLING

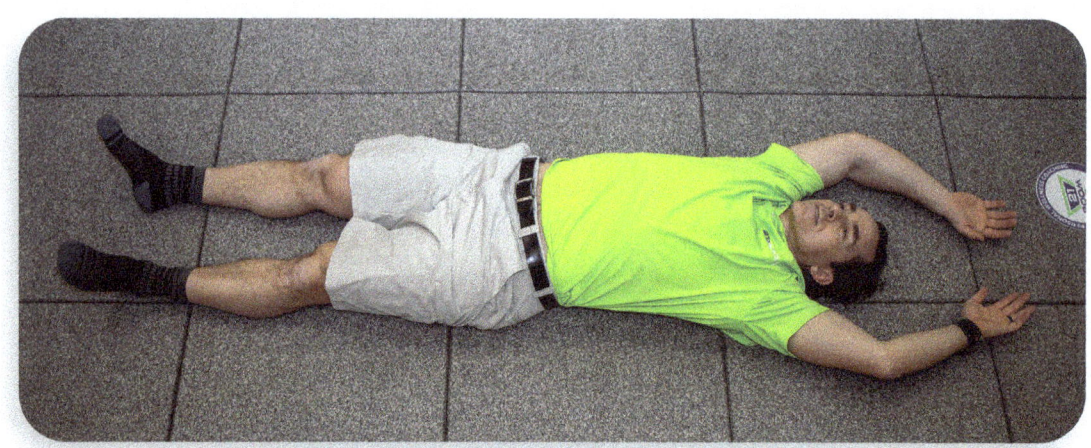

Exercise Description:

This exercise will reflexively activate some of the deepest midsection muscles you have. Begin by lying on your back. Lift one leg and bring it across your body. Lift your head and look in the direction you are rolling. Using your midsection muscles, slowly roll to your stomach while leading with the leg. Once on your stomach, lift one leg, look in the direction you are rolling, and bring the leg across your body.

HEAD NOD (side to side)

 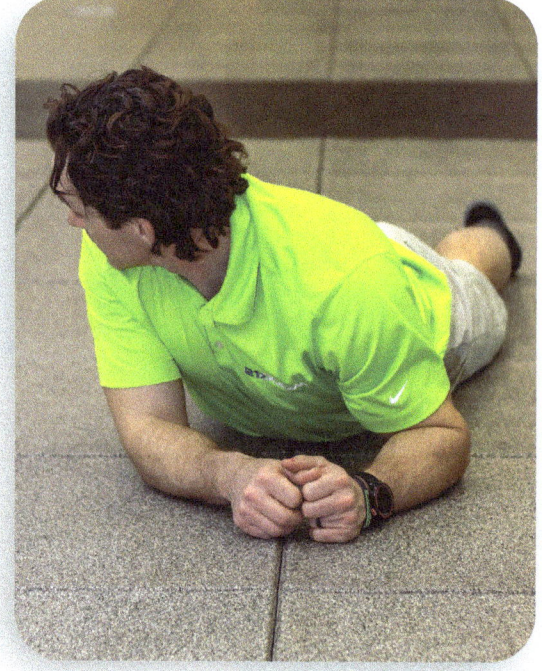

Exercise Description:

People who do not move their heads and necks are not well. Let's connect your body through head nods. You can execute head nods in any body position. Lie on your stomach and gaze forward with your chin on an imaginary shelf. Slide your chin onto that shelf and bring your gaze behind you, paying attention to the connection between your torso, neck, and head. Repeat for the other side.

HIP ROCK

Exercise Description:

Just as you experienced when you were a baby, you will mobilize your hips and connect your body reflexively. Begin in a tabletop position, then widen your knees and sit on your heels. Extend your arms and begin hip-rocking forward. When your hips reach full extension, return to the starting position and repeat.

SINGLE LEG HIP ROCK

Exercise Description:

From the hip-rock position, extend one leg directly to the side. Rock your hips forward and backward as you feel a stretch of your inner hip musculature.

SIDE-TO-SIDE PIGEON POSE

Exercise Description:

Begin in a tabletop position. Lift your knees and slide one leg up and through so that the outer aspect of the leg is in contact with the floor. You'll experience a glute stretch when you sit the hips down and extend the opposite leg. This is a great time to add another head nod.

ACTIVE STRAIGHT LEG RAISE CORRECTIVE

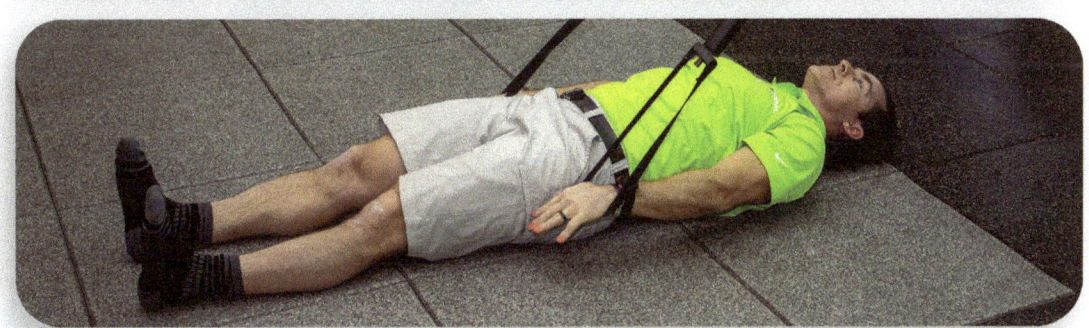

Exercise Description:

Use a Cook Band or other resistance band. Lie on your back with legs and arms extended. Bring your hands with the band to your hips. Keeping your legs locked and toes tucked toward your knees, lift one leg as far as you can. Return the leg to the ground and bring your arms back to the starting position.

GLUTE BRIDGE

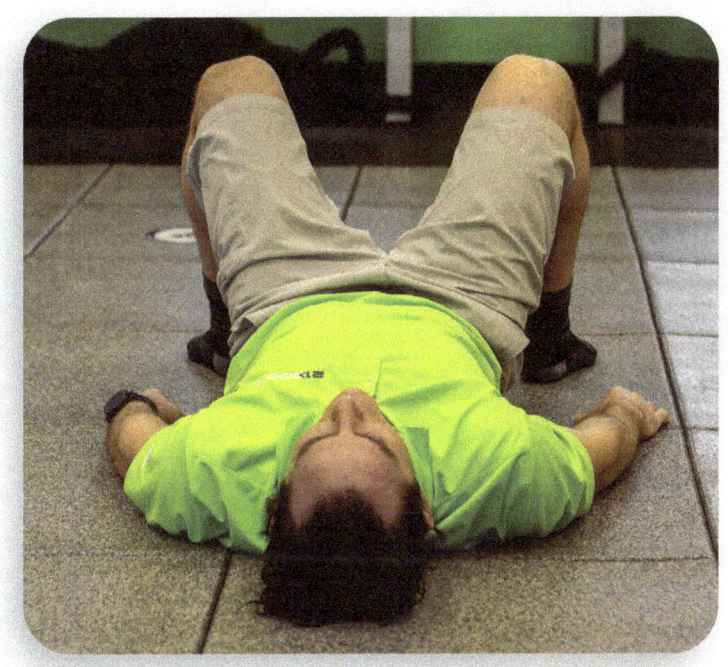

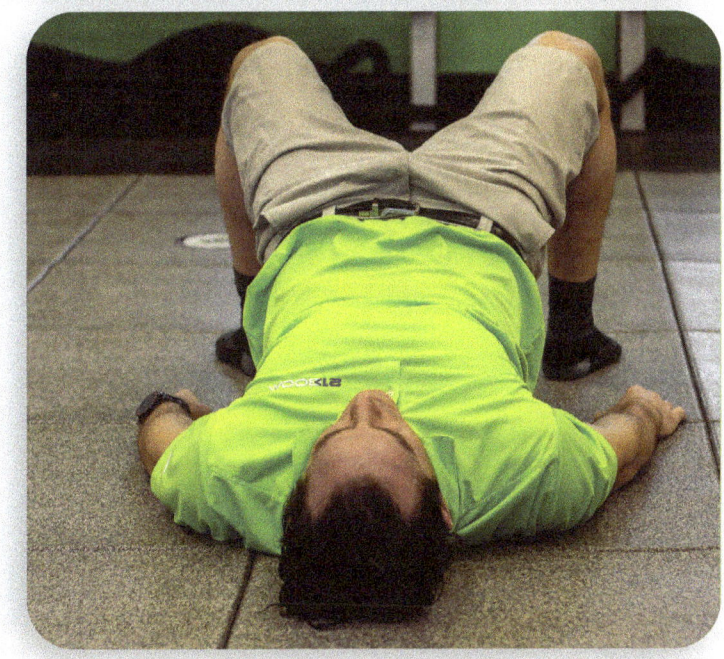

Exercise Description:

Lie on your back with your knees bent. Lift your hips to full hip extension and return to the ground.

MODIFIED SIDE PLANK

Exercise Description:

Lie on your side with knees bent at 90°. Lift your hips and remain in a neutral spine. Hold for the recommended amount of time. To increase the intensity, extend your legs so your feet become the endpoint and not the knees.

MULTIDIRECTIONAL MARCHING

Exercise Description:

Stand tall. Begin lifting one knee while bringing the opposite arm upward. Return to the starting position and continue this contralateral motion in any direction. Forward, backward, and side-to-side marching all enhance the vestibular system.

DIAPHRAGM WAKEUP DRILL

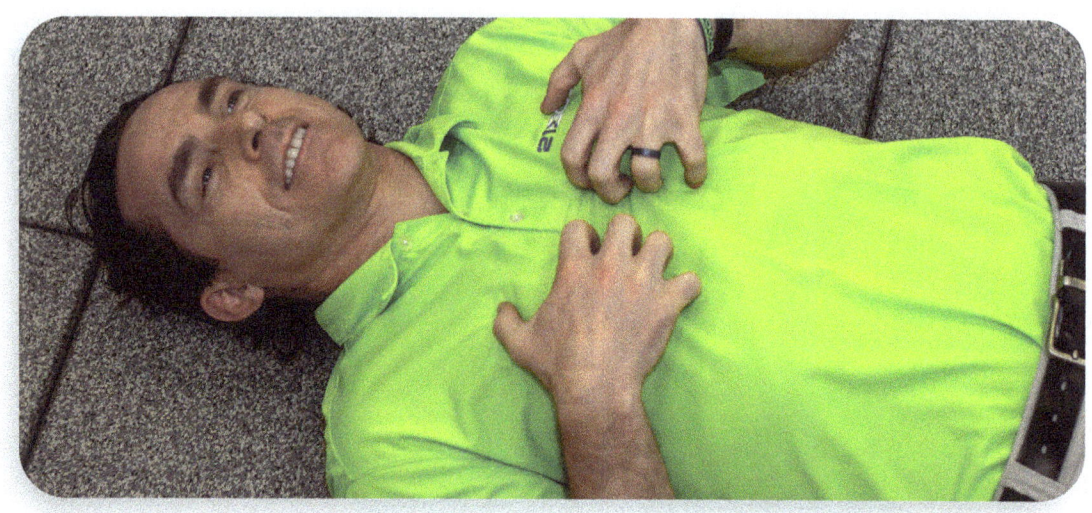

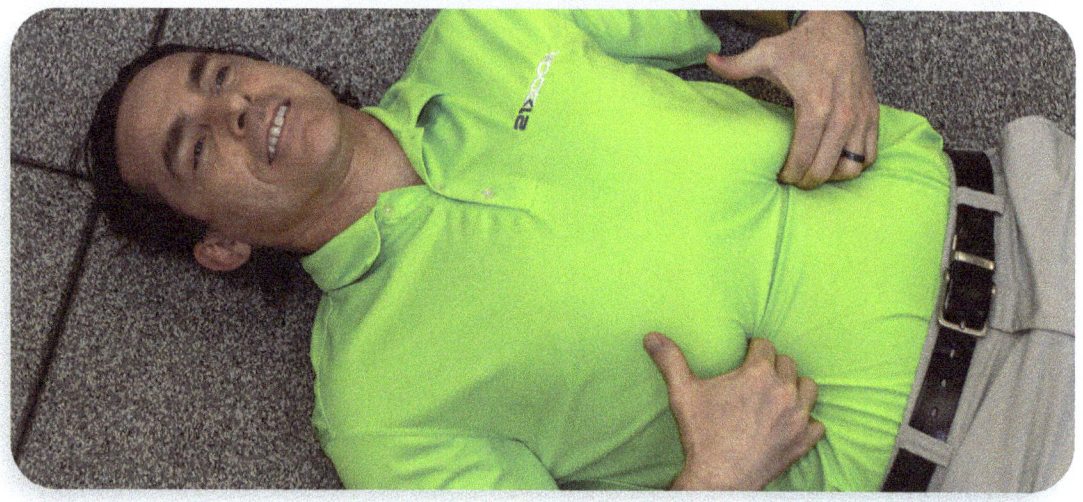

Exercise Description:

To improve your body's ability to move better through breathing efficiency, lie on your back, relax, and diaphragmatically breathe. Begin rubbing into your sternum with one or two hands (using the tips of your fingers). Next, find the base of your rib cage. Begin digging laterally under the bottom of the ribs. Pay attention to any tenderness and tightness of the diaphragm. Relax and breathe through the wakeup drills.

UPPER BODY SEGMENTAL ROLLING

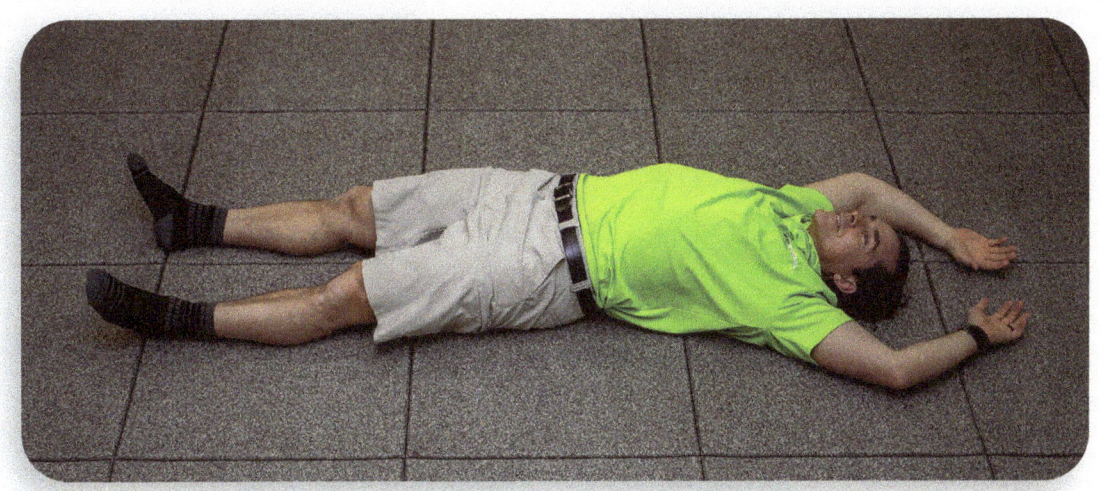

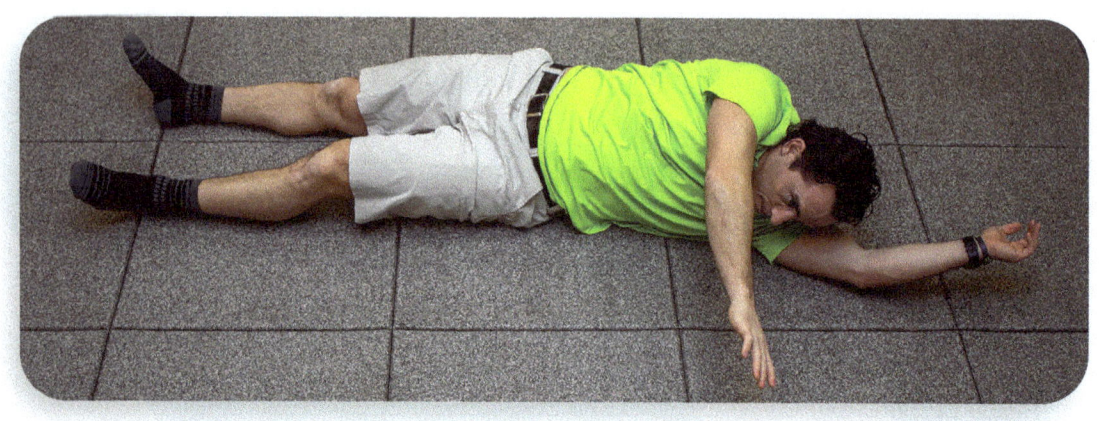

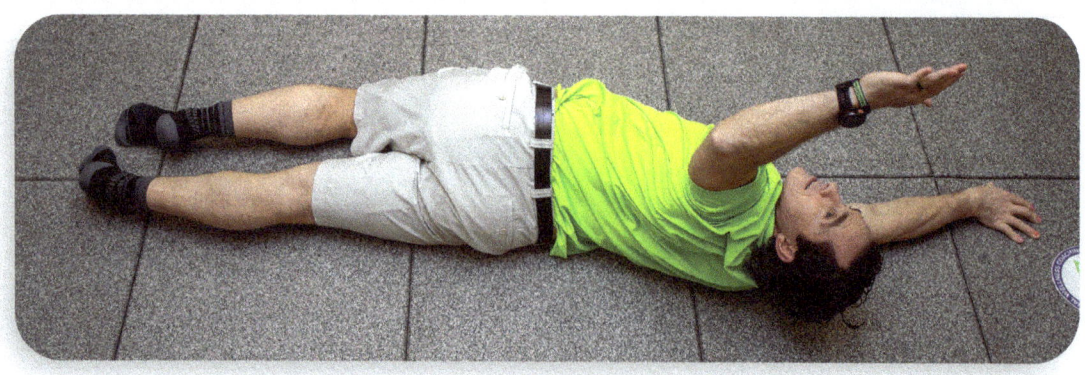

Exercise Description:

Begin by lying on your back. Lift one arm and bring it across your body. Lift your head and look in the direction you are rolling. Using your midsection muscles, slowly roll to your stomach while leading with the arm. Once on your stomach, lift one arm, look in the direction you are rolling, and bring the arm behind and across your body. Using your midsection muscles, slowly roll to your back. Be sure to keep all muscles below the waist relaxed.

HEAD NOD (Up and Down)

Exercise Description:

You can execute head nods in any body position. Lie on your stomach, gazing forward. Look to the ceiling and let the head follow the eyes upward. Once at the top of a comfortable range of motion, look down toward the ground and let the head follow the eyes.

HALF KNEELING ROCKING

Exercise Description:

Begin in a half-kneeling position. Swing the top leg 90°. Lean over the top leg, feeling a stretch of the adductors of the hip. You can also keep the foot in front, lean forward, and feel the hip muscles stretch.

PLANK OR MODIFIED PLANK

Exercise Description:

Lie on your stomach with your elbows under your shoulders and toes tucked. Bring your hips and knees off the ground so that your body is in a neutral spine position. Maintain this position for the recommended duration. Enhance core stability with increased time under tension.

PASSIVE LEG LOWERING

Exercise Description:

Find the corner of a wall. Lie on your back with one leg on the wall. Keep both legs fully extended with toes tucked toward the knees. Slowly begin lifting the down leg to an upright position, then return to the starting position.

CROSS CRAWL

Exercise Description:

Stand tall with arms extended to the ceiling. Lift one knee while bringing the opposite arm to that knee, then return to the starting position. Alternate sides in a contralateral fashion.

PSOAS WAKEUP DRILL

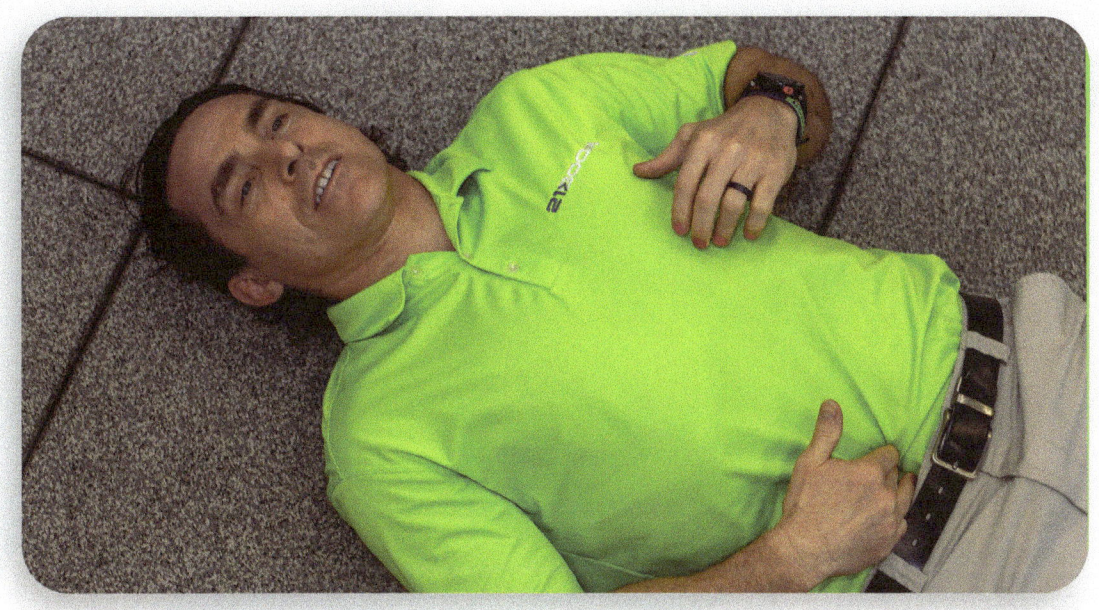

Exercise Description:

Lie on your back and find your belly button. Measure one inch over and one inch down and begin pushing in the fingers of one hand at a 45° angle. Place the opposite hand on top of that hand to add pressure and move the fingers in a small circle.

HARD ROLLING

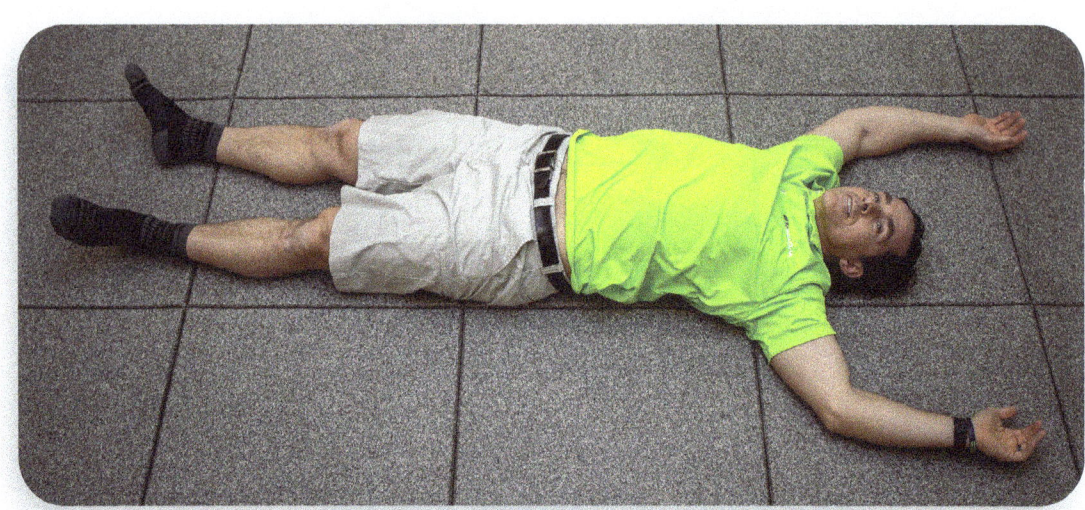

Exercise Description:

Lie on your back with your arms and legs fully extended. Lift your arms, legs, head, and shoulders off the ground. Look in the direction you want to roll, and using your midsection muscles, roll to your side and eventually to your stomach. While on your stomach, lift your extended arms and legs, look in the direction you want to roll, and using your midsection muscles, roll to your side and eventually to your back.

DEAD BUG

Exercise Description:

Lie on your back with your arms extended toward the ceiling and legs off the ground in a 90° hip and knee position. Bring one hand to the opposite knee while extending the opposite arm and leg. Return arms and legs to the starting position and repeat or alternate in a contralateral pattern.

HURDLE STEP CORRECTIVE

Exercise Description:

Attach a Cook Band or other resistance band to a stable pivot point. Stand tall while grasping the band. Bring your arms to your hips, hold, breathe, and lift one knee. Return the foot to the ground and repeat or alternate legs while maintaining arm position and core activation.

BABY CRAWLS

Exercise Description:

Begin in a tabletop position. Move your hand and opposite leg in a contra-lateral pattern as you baby-crawl forward, backward, or from side to side.

LEOPARD CRAWLS

Exercise Description:

Begin in a tabletop position with your toes tucked. Lift your knees barely off the ground. Move your hand and opposite leg in a contra-lateral pattern as you leopard-crawl forward, backward, or from side to side. Keep your spine in neutral and your hips stable, and envision crawling like a prowling cat.

SPIDER CRAWLS

Exercise Description:

The spider crawl is similar to a leopard crawl. Begin in a tabletop position with your toes tucked. Lift your knees barely off the ground and flare them to the sides as you crawl. Move your hand and opposite leg in a contralateral pattern as you spider-crawl forward, backward, or from side to side. Keep your spine in neutral and your hips stable, and envision scaling a rock cliff.

BIRD DOG

Exercise Description:

Begin in a tabletop position. Extend your arm and opposite leg fully in a contralateral pattern as you bird dog–crawl forward, backward, or from side to side.

GLUTE WAKEUP DRILL

Exercise Description:

Enhancing the reflexive neural connection to your glutes provides many benefits such as better movement, enhanced metabolism, and reduced risk of injury. Bring your thumbs to the posterior aspect of the base of your skull. Scrape the soft tissue laterally, paying attention to any tenderness or tension.

HALF-KNEELING PALLOF PRESS

Exercise Description:

Pallof-press in any stance. Position a resistance band at chest height while in half-kneeling position. Grab the band with one hand and the opposite hand on top at chest level. Place appropriate tension on the band and extend your arms. Pause and bring your hands back to the starting position.

STANDING HIP HINGE

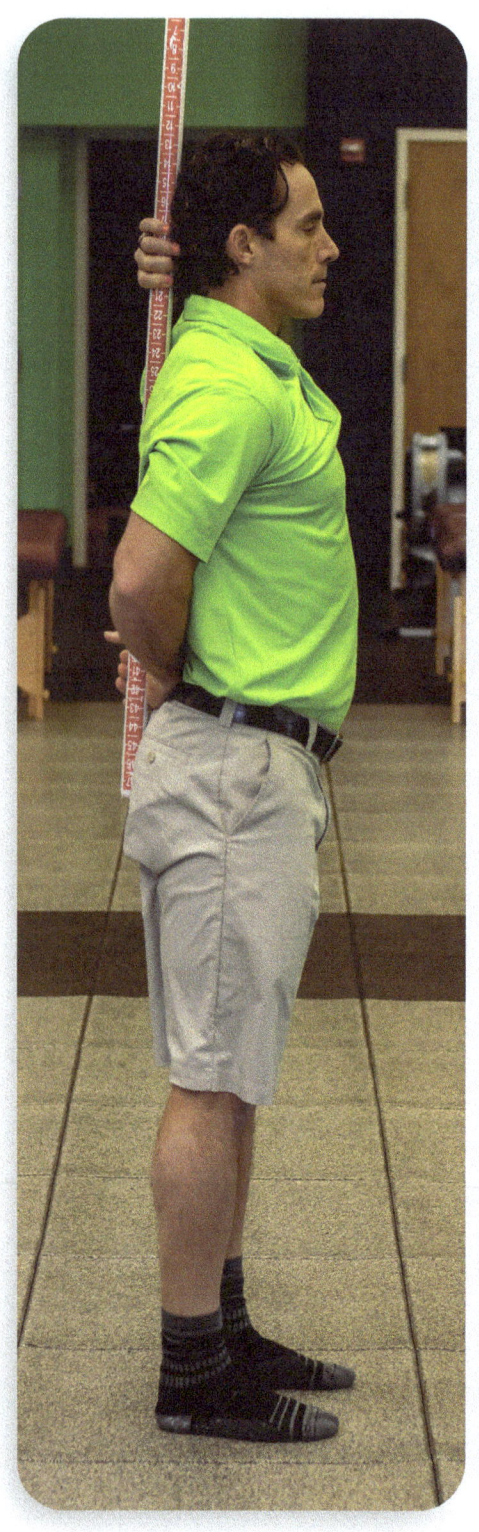

Exercise Description:

Stand tall with a shoulder-width stance. Place a dowel on three attachment points: your lower back, your upper back, and your head. Position one hand in the lordosis of your cervical spine and the other in the lordosis of your lumbar spine and slowly begin bringing your hips back (hip-hinging). At the same time, move your upper torso in direct opposition toward the floor. Maintain a neutral spine and comfortably bent knees.

Hinge at the hips through a full range of motion, then return to the starting position.

You can load this movement when appropriate by using a band. Attach a band to a low attachment point and straddle the band.

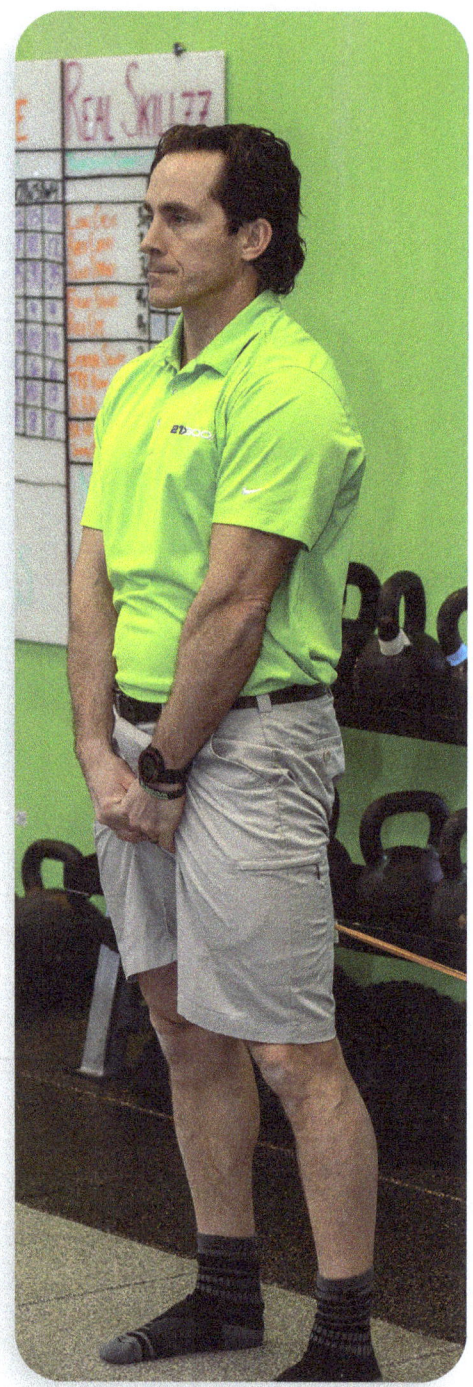

TOE-TOUCH PROGRESSION ON 1/2 FOAM ROLLER

Exercise Description:

Place your toes on the top of a 1/2 foam roller. Extend your arms to the ceiling, relax, breathe, and begin hip-hinging by bringing your hips back and your arms toward your toes. Continue transitioning your hands to your toes by shifting your hips back, emphasizing an anterior pelvic tilt, chin tuck, and spine flexion. Bend your knees as much as you need to touch your toes, then return to the starting position successfully.

DYNAMIC MOVEMENT FLOWS
CROSS LEG TAP

Exercise Description:

Stand tall, then lift one leg fully extended while touching with the opposite hand.

ANKLE GRAB

Exercise Description:

Stand tall, grab one ankle, pull into the glute, push the hips forward, and reach toward the ceiling with the opposite arm.

SINGLE LEG HIP HINGE

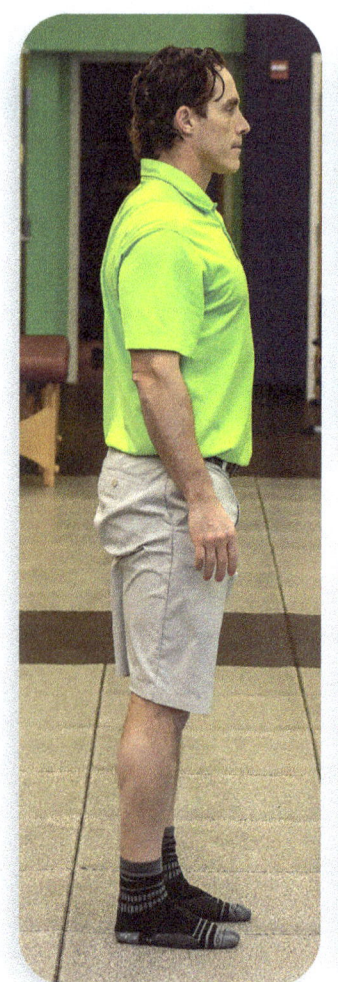

Exercise Description:

Keep one foot on the ground while you aggressively hip-hinge. Move your torso as close to parallel to the floor as you can comfortably.

ANKLE GRAB WITH HIP HINGE

DYNAMIC GLUTE STRETCH

Exercise Description:

Stand tall and cross one leg over the other knee. Sit and feel a glute stretch. You can also grab the foot and knee simultaneously to feel a glute stretch.

HAMSTRING

Exercise Description:

Stand tall and extend one leg with heel down and toe up. Hip-hinge aggressively and maintain a neutral spine.

LATERAL SLING WAKEUP DRILL

Exercise Description:

Lie on your back. Find the top of your hip with each thumb. Begin scraping the edge of the entire hip. Wakeup drills feel uncomfortable, so try to relax and breathe as you dig in.

RESISTED PUSH TOE TOUCH

 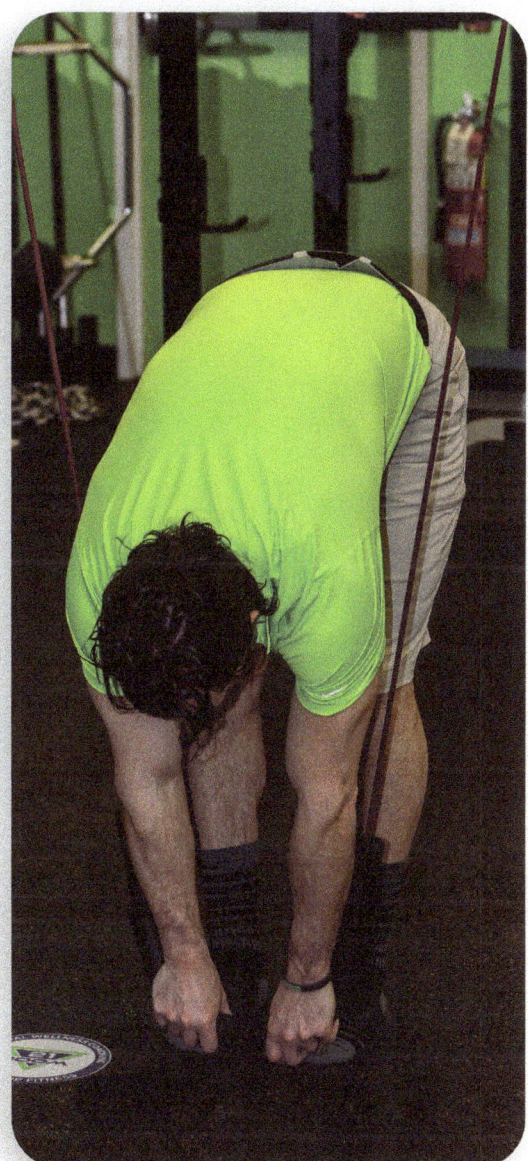

Exercise Description:

Set a resistance band at the knee to hip height. Perform a toe touch and push against the band as you touch your toes. This movement activates your core and should help you to pattern the toe touch. Another variation of this toe touch is to squeeze an object, such as a yoga block, between the thighs as you pattern the toe touch.

RESIST-A-BALL ISOMETRIC CORE STABILITY

Exercise Description:

Lie on your back with your arms extended toward the ceiling and your hips and knees bent at 90°. You can use a stability ball to bring all extremities in toward each other. This exercise is an isometric exercise with many options. You can activate spiral lines with opposite arms and legs, obliques with the same side arm and leg, and the entire core with all extremities.

SINGLE LEG ROMANIAN DEADLIFT

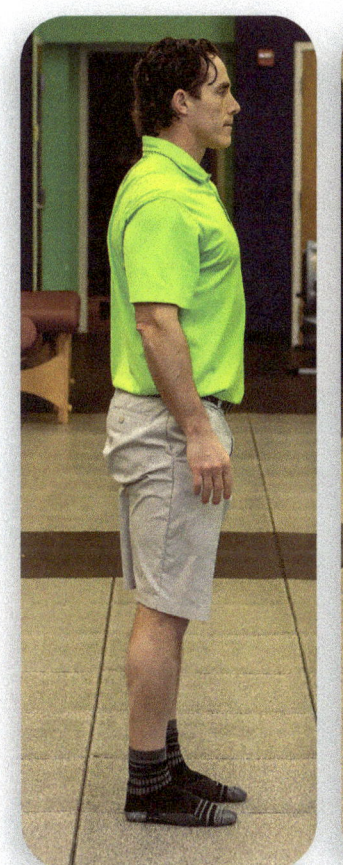

Exercise Description:

Stand tall. Begin by bringing one leg behind you as you hip-hinge aggressively. Slowly hinge and move your torso as close to parallel to the ground as possible. This exercise can be done with or without load.

PERPENDICULAR PASSIVE POSTURE CORRECTIVE

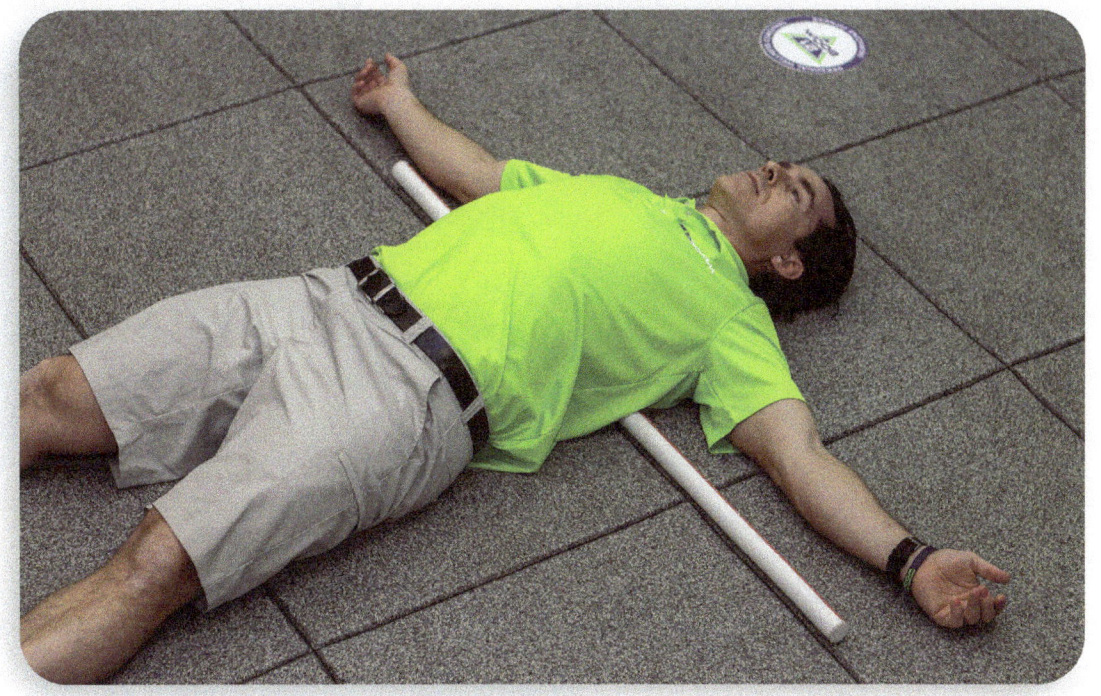

Exercise Description:

Lie on your back with a dowel or small cylindrical object perpendicular to your thoracic spine. Be sure the object is not too large. Relax and breathe and let your spine extend around the object. Periodically move the dowel higher on the spine one vertebrae at a time.

PARALLEL PASSIVE POSTURE CORRECTIVE ON FOAM ROLLER W/BREATH

Exercise Description:

Lie on a foam roller with your elbows at a 90° angle. Relax and breathe.

MYOFASCIAL PREPARATION—ENTIRE BACK-SIDE CHAIN

NECK

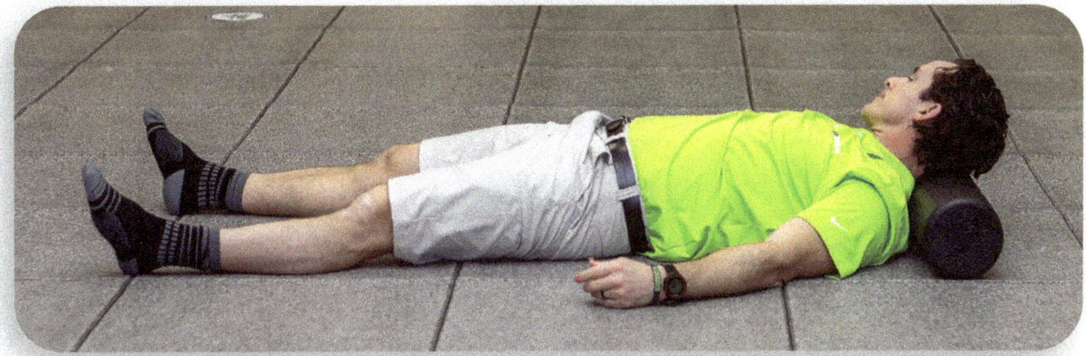

THORACIC SPINE

LATS

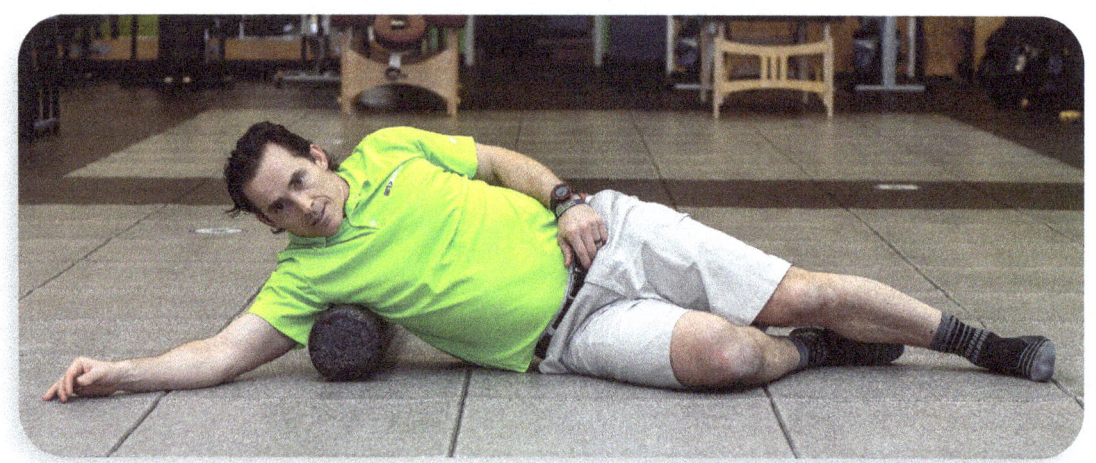

GLUTES

CALVES

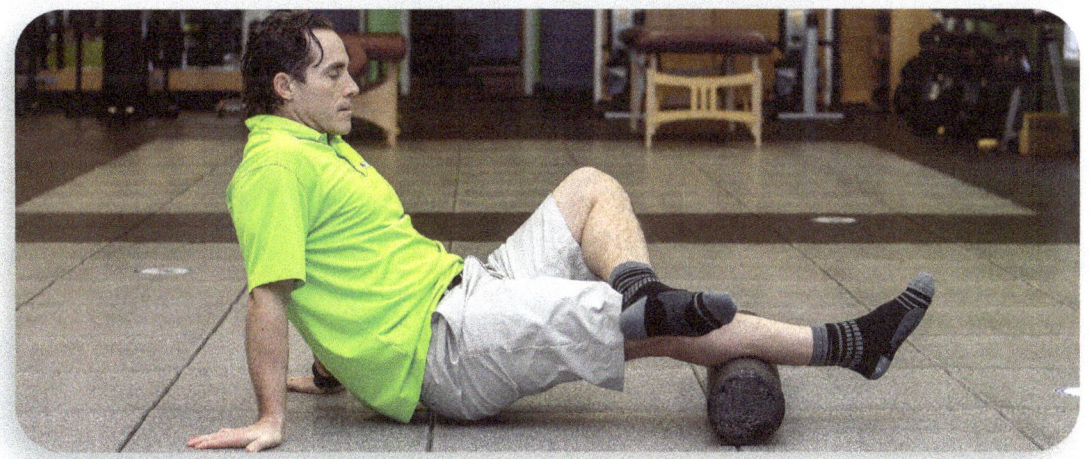

Exercise Description:

Muscles tend to tighten and develop neural abnormalities through training, stress, excessive sitting, or poor biomechanics. Myofascial release places pressure on muscles, creating a reflexive response that aids in proper muscle function. Use a foam roll, stick, or massage to put pressure on muscles of the backside chain. These muscles tend to tighten through daily living. Breathe and relax as you "roll" and place pressure on tight muscles and tender points.

FOAM ROLL THORACIC EXTENSION

Exercise Description:

Lie perpendicular with your thoracic spine on a foam roller. Hold your head in your hands and bring your elbows closer. Gently lift your elbows, extending your spine, then return to the starting position.

SKYDIVER

Exercise Description:

Lie on your stomach with your arms and legs at 45° angles, much like a star. Lift your arms, legs, and head off the ground, so your backside muscles are activated. Hold this position and breathe. Avoid excessive extension of the spine.

SHOULDER WAKE UP DRILL

Exercise Description:

Lie on your back and reach one hand across your body on your ribs. Position your hand as if it were a tiger claw and scrape or pull the hand across your rib cage. Repeat.

SUPRASPINATUS WAKEUP DRILL

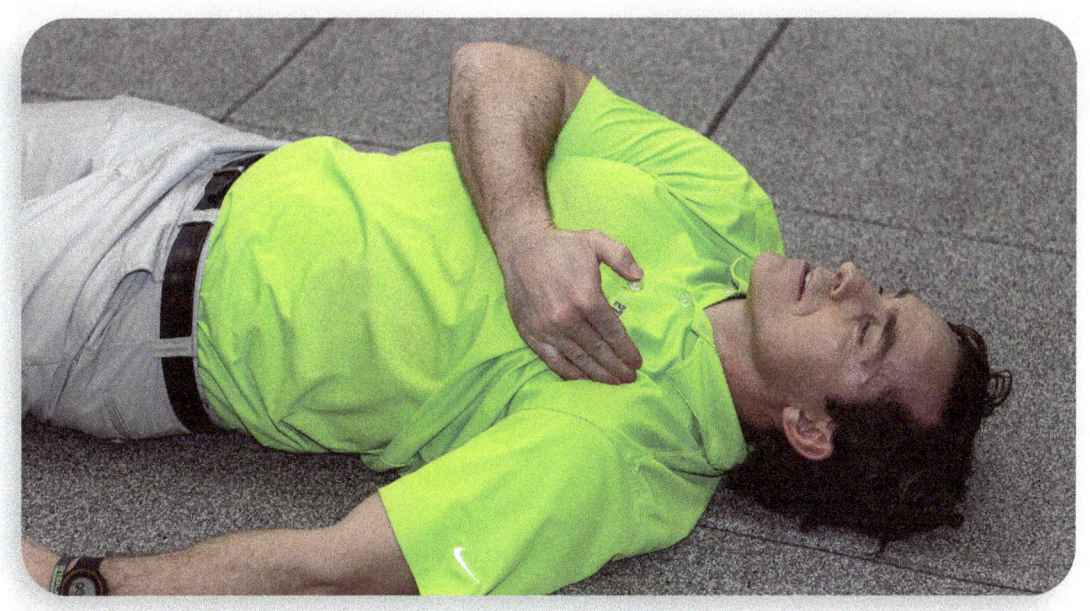

Exercise Description:

Position your hand as a saw and place on the front of your shoulder where your arm meets your torso. Begin "sawing" the soft tissue.

NECK WAKEUP DRILL

Exercise Description:

Find your clavicle bones with the tips of your fingers. Begin scraping just beneath the clavicles with one or both hands.

MYOFASCIAL PREP—AROUND SHOULDER

TOOLS

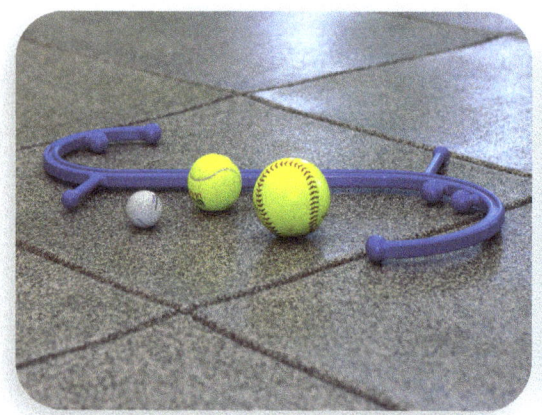

LATISSIMUS DORSI
DELTOIDS

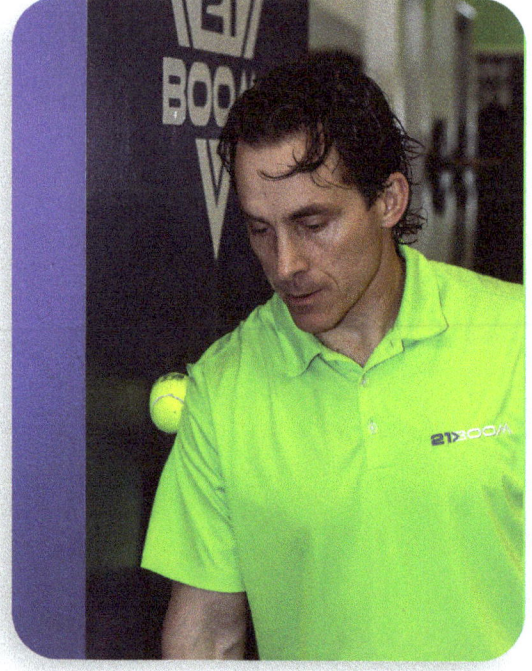

CHEST/SHOULDERS

Exercise Description:

Find a wall or doorway and place your hands above your shoulders in the doorway or on the wall. Lean forward and stretch the chest and shoulders.

ARM SWEEPS

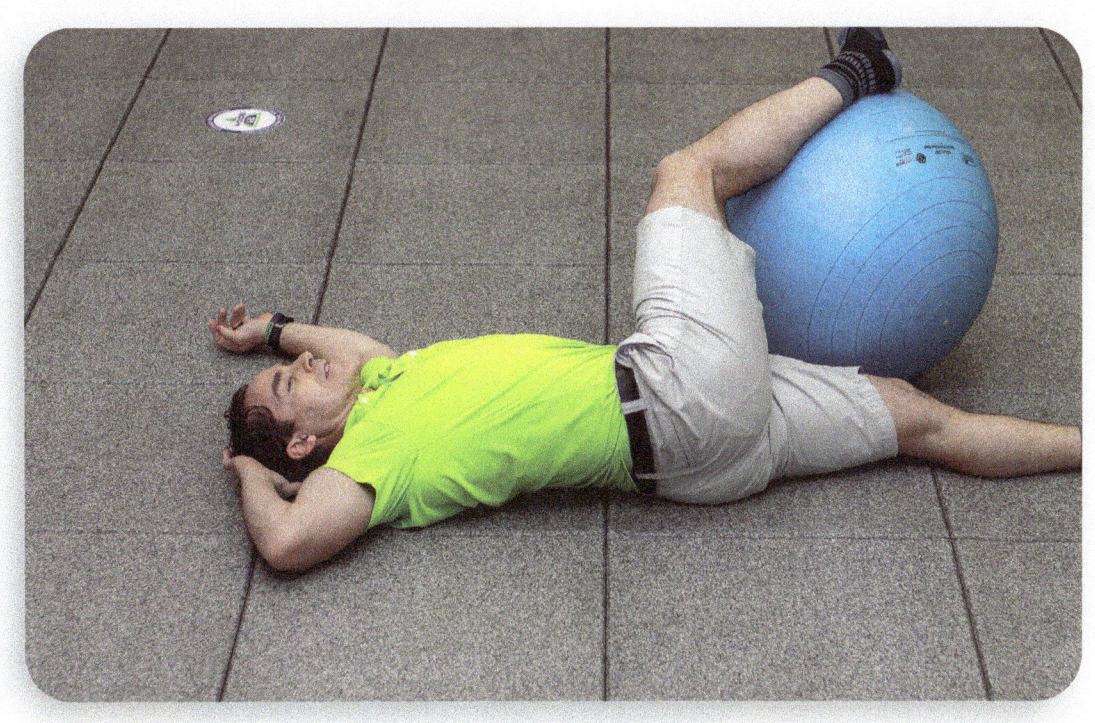

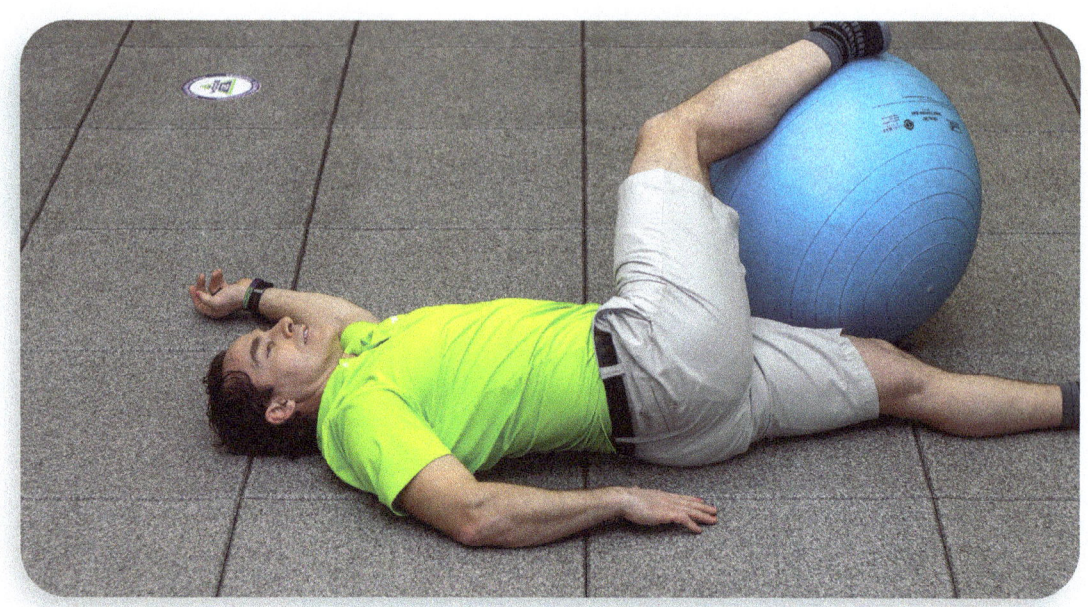

Exercise Description:

Lie on your back with one leg across your body on a platform or stability ball. Extend your opposite arm fully with your upper back on the ground. Begin "sweeping" the arm from the top of your head to your lower back. You should try to keep your shoulders, elbow, and wrist on the ground during this sweeping motion. When your arm transitions toward your back, keep your palm down. When your arm is transitioning toward your head, keep your palm up.

INDIAN CLUBS

Exercise Description:

Use Indian clubs to enhance the mobility of your shoulder joints. Indian clubs provide traction of the shoulder joints during circular motions. Play with this and have fun!

LATS WAKEUP DRILL

Exercise Description:

Locate the base of your rib cage. Move up three ribs and locate a slight indentation of the rib cage. Drill in with your thumb while you breathe and relax.

FOAM ROLL THORACIC SPINE

Exercise Description:

Place your thoracic spine perpendicular to a foam roll with your hands supporting your head. Roll back and forth through the mid-spine.

QUADRUPED T-SPINE ROTATION
HAND ON NECK OR HAND ON LOWER BACK PALM UP

Exercise Description:

This exercise can be done with the hand behind the head or arm extended. Start in a tabletop position. Sit on your heels and place one hand behind your head. Begin rotating toward the ceiling with your eyes and elbow. When you reach a full range of motion, begin turning toward the opposite hand and repeat.

BRETTZEL

Exercise Description:

Lie on your side and grab your lower leg/ankle with your topside hand. Bring your back and shoulders to the ground as you bend your topside leg. Position your bottom-side hand on your topside knee. Breathe and relax as you hold this stretch.

GASTROCNEMIUS WAKEUP DRILL

Exercise Description:

Lie on your side. Using your thumb, find a point just below your rib cage toward your belly button on your front side. On the other hand, using the thumb, find a position on the back that is directly in opposition to your front-side point. Drill your thumbs toward each other.

MYOFASCIAL PREP—PLANTAR FASCIA

Exercise Description:

Use a golf ball or object that provides appropriate pressure for your plantar fascia. Place your foot on the object and massage the entire plantar fascia.

PASSIVE FOOT RANGE OF MOTION

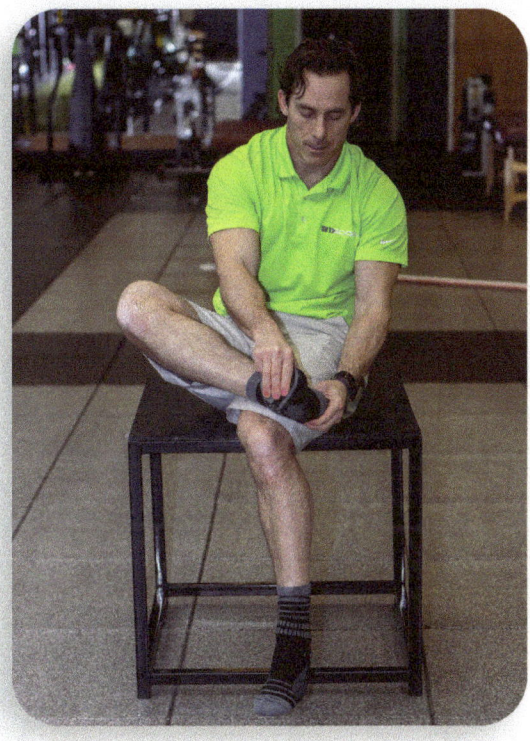

Exercise Description:

Use your hands to stretch the joints of the foot in flexion and extension. These joints include the ankle, interphalangeal joints, metatarsophalangeal joints, and tarsometatarsal joints.

ACTIVE FOOT RANGE OF MOTION

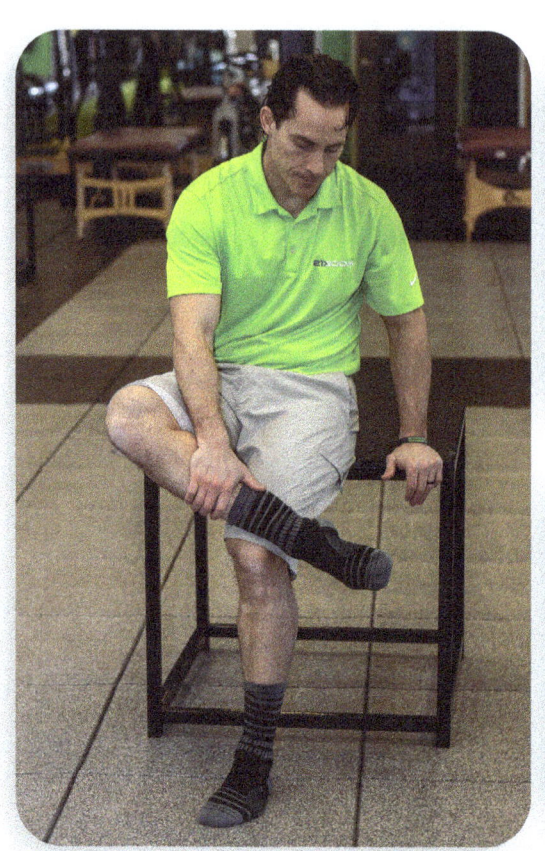
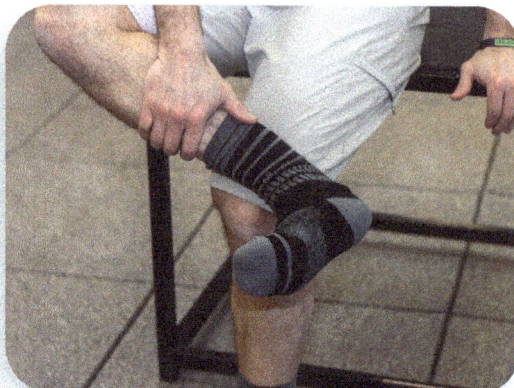
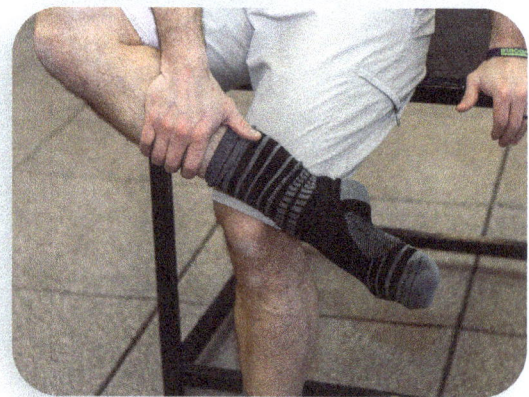

Exercise Description:

Move your foot and ankle through a full flexion and extension range of motion.

GASTROCNEMIUS/ANKLE STRETCH

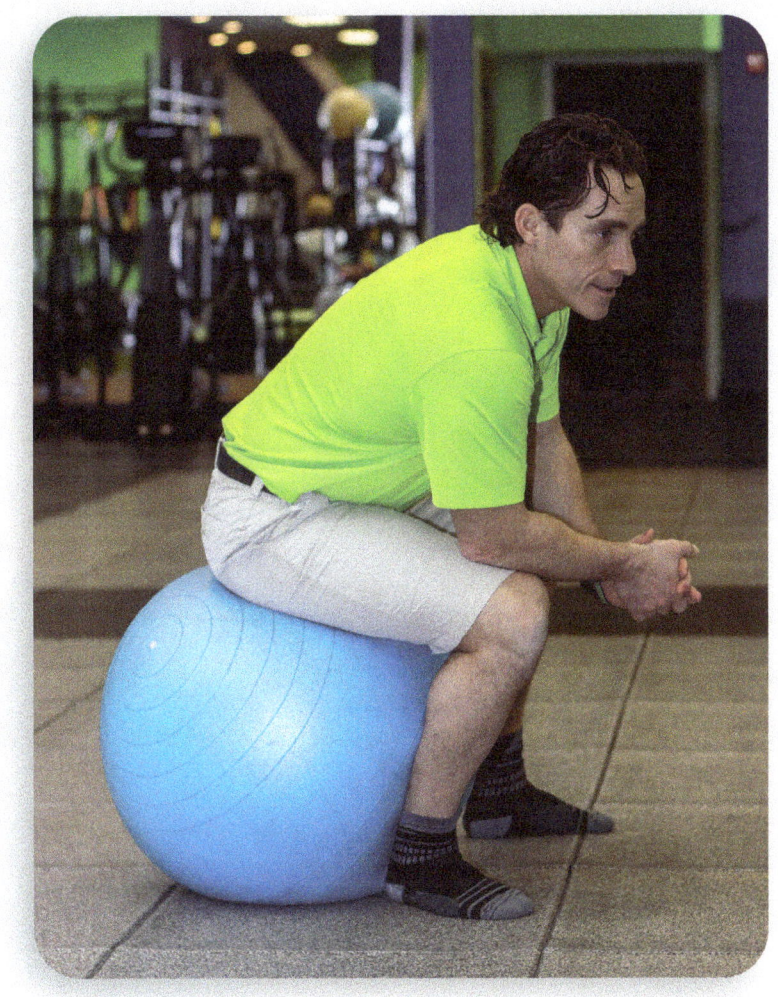

Exercise Description:

Sit on a stability ball. Bring one heel into the stability ball as far as possible. Begin shifting your body weight over the heel to stretch the soft tissue of the lower posterior leg.

ABDOMINAL WAKEUP DRILL

Exercise Description:

Chop the inside of your legs from your knees to your groin.

ASSISTED DEEP SQUAT PATTERNING

Exercise Description:

Find a pole. Begin in a squat stance with your hands on the pole. Slide your hands down the pole as you squat toward your ankles. Maintain a neutral spine, keep your heels on the ground, relax, and breathe. Pause at the bottom, then return to the starting position.

SQUAT PATTERNING WITH BODY WEIGHT

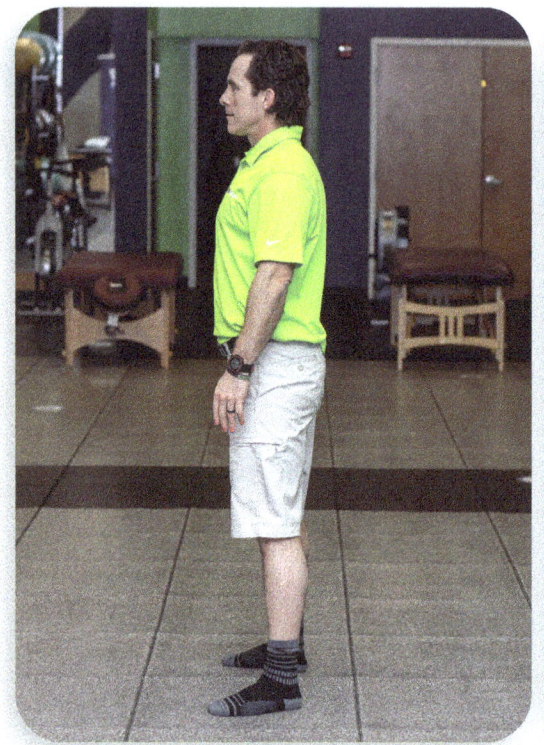

Exercise Description:

Start in a squat stance (feet slightly wider than shoulder-width with your toes pointed out comfortably) with your arms extended for a counterbalance. Initiate the movement with your hips and begin squatting. Try to keep your torso upright and spine in neutral as you squat. Your thighs are parallel to the ground at the bottom of the squat. Return to the starting position by driving your hips, standing tall, and swimming the arms to your hips. Get your breath in sequence with the movement pattern by exhaling on exertion. You should feel your glutes and core activation at the top of the squat pattern.

QUADRICEPS WAKEUP DRILL

Exercise Description:

Lie on your back. Find the space between the top of your hip and the bottom of your rib cage. Using your thumb as a hook, begin pulling the tissue across the body repeatedly. Wakeup drills feel uncomfortable, so try to relax and breathe as you dig in.

WALL ANGELS (FLOOR OR WALL)

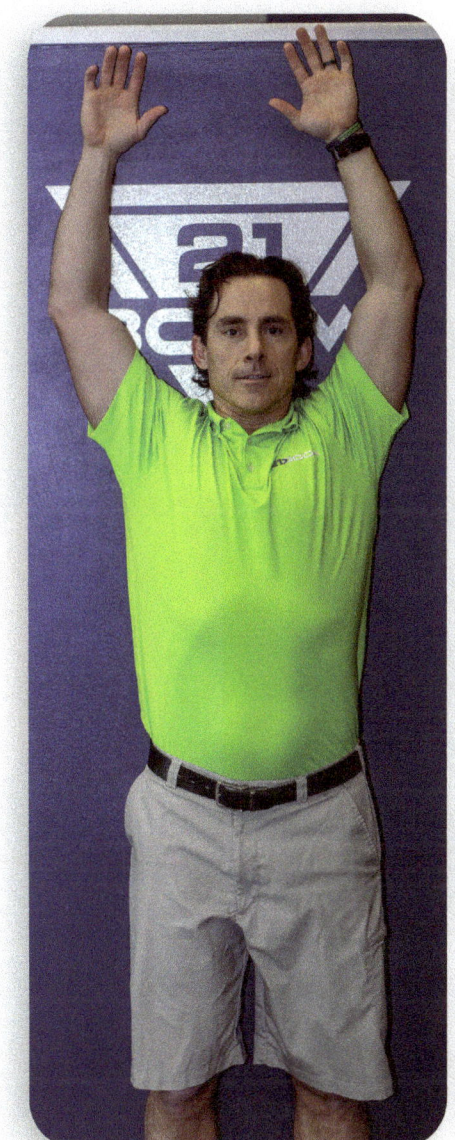

Exercise Description:

You can perform this exercise on a wall or the floor. Position your arms in a goalpost position with your elbows at 90°. Keep your elbows and wrists on the wall (or floor) and begin moving your arms upward. Go through a full range of motion, then return to the starting position.

MILESTONE INFOGRAPHIC

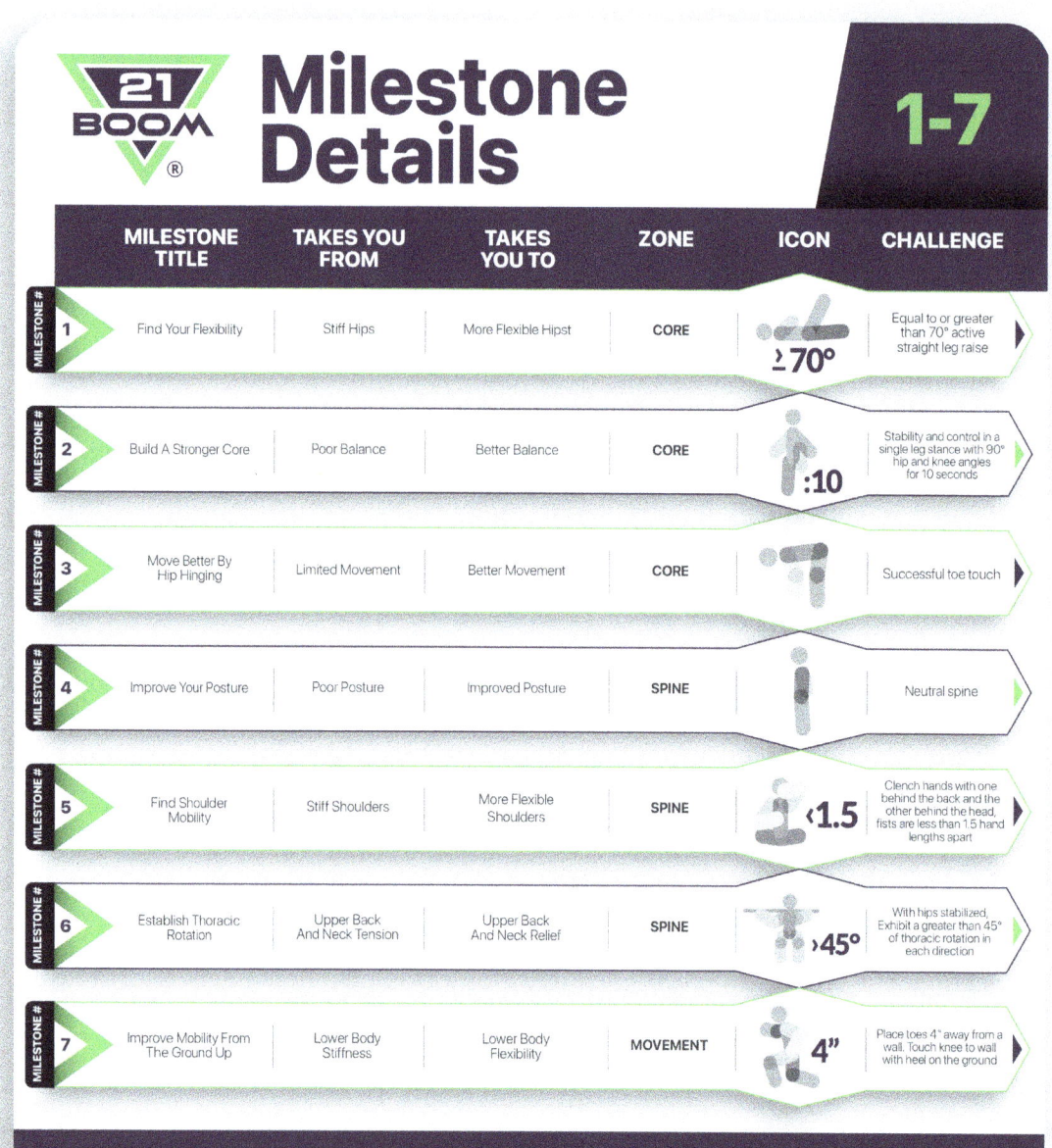

Milestone Details 8-14

MILESTONE	MILESTONE TITLE	TAKES YOU FROM	TAKES YOU TO	ZONE	ICON	CHALLENGE
MILESTONE # 8	Pattern The Squat	Poor Foot To Core Sequencing	Proficient Foot To Core Sequencing	MOVEMENT		Pattern a squat with upper leg parallel to the ground with hands overhead
MILESTONE # 9	Apply The Squat And Connect To Strength	Connect To Strength Squat Patterning	Loading The Squat	MOVEMENT	25%	Pattern a squat with 25% of your body weight
MILESTONE # 10	Train The Five Human Movements	Unaware of Natural Movement	Moving Naturally	TRANSFORMATION	5	5-minute leopard crawl
MILESTONE # 11	Develop Kettlebell Skills	Minimal Skills	Effective Variety of Skills	TRANSFORMATION	Skills	Prove proficiency with a Kettlebell deadlift, press, swing, clean, snatch, and Turkish Get Up
MILESTONE # 12	Be Consistent To Look And Feel Better	Current Body Composition	Improved Body Composition	TRANSFORMATION	▼%FAT	Lower % body fat
MILESTONE # 13	Create More Strength And Power	Current Strength	Stronger All Around	PERFORMANCE	7 1/2	7:30-minute leopard crawl
MILESTONE # 14	Develop Double Kettlebell Skills To Crush Your Workouts	Single Kettlebell Skills	Proficient With Double Kettlebell Skills	PERFORMANCE	Skills	Prove proficiency with a double Kettlebell squat, press, swing, clean, and snatch

www.21-boom.com

Milestone Details 15-21

MILESTONE #	MILESTONE TITLE	TAKES YOU FROM	TAKES YOU TO	ZONE	ICON	CHALLENGE
15	Confidence Is The Best Payoff	Improved Body Composition	Ideal Body Composition	PERFORMANCE	▼%FAT	Lower % body fat
16	Link The Unbreakable Chain	Stronger	Greater Strength & Power	PEAK PERFORMANCE	10	10-minute leopard crawl
17	Activate Peak Performance	Fit	As Fit As You Have Ever Been	PEAK PERFORMANCE	100 / 5min	100 single arm snatch repetitions in 5 minutes with 1 kettlebell lower than your snatch weight kettlebell
18	Looking In The Mirror Never Looked So Good	Great Workouts	More Than Just A Workout	PEAK PERFORMANCE	▼%FAT	Lower % body fat
19	Maintain Peak Performance	Performing Well	Peak Performance And Injury Resilience	EXTRAORDINARY LIVING	▶10	MOVE FORWARD EVENT: 10-Minute Leopard Crawl
20	Live The Active Life And Win	As Fit As You Have Ever Been	Achieving The Greatest Physical Accomplishments of Your Life	EXTRAORDINARY LIVING	🏆	MOVE FORWARD EVENT: Pass the Snatch Test
21	Respect The Practice And The Process	Respecting The Practice And The Process	Living The Active Life And Setting An Example For Others	EXTRAORDINARY LIVING	▽	MOVE FORWARD EVENT: Set a Life Goal

www.21-boom.com

www.ingramcontent.com/pod-product-compliance
Lightning Source LLC
Chambersburg PA
CBHW040930240426
43672CB00021B/2992